A Full Circle

"Anyone who has ever wondered where a journey into their soul would lead will be moved and inspired by Debra's story. I was amazed at how in finding her own voice, she created the space to be the voice for many girls and women. In a world in which it truly "takes a village" Debra inspired women to be the village it would take to move subsequent generations of girls forward."

—Anita Janssen, Effectiveness Coach

"God has a plan for each of us and he is obviously using Debra as a bridge between the Maasai women of Tanzania and those whose hearts are tugged by the stories in this book."

—Liz Mach, Maryknoll Lay Missioners,
serving Africa/Tanzania for thirty-five years

"The inspiring journey in *A Full Circle* is a good reminder to all of us to follow our hearts as well as our inner voice. I've been lucky enough to travel to Tanzania twice with Debra and have seen firsthand how the IMAGE Project has helped Masaai women and girls courageously tap into their own empowerment and voice. One person's commitment really can make a difference in the lives of others."

—Linda Cullen, founder/director
of Fifty Lanterns International

"Debra shares the compelling personal stories of Maasai women overcoming remarkable obstacles to obtain an education, while they live in a culture that values women based on how hard they can work or the cost of a cow. The women's fierce determination to improve life for themselves, their mothers, their sisters, and their country is inspiring. As you travel with Debra on her life-changing journey, you will meet these girls, hear their stories, and never forget them."

—Whitney R. Bischoff, DrPH, RN,
associate professor of nursing,
Texas A&M International University

"This story reminds us that the best way to make a difference in the world is by building genuine relationships with people over time. Despite enormous cultural and linguistic differences, the author meets the women of Kwale with humility and willingness to listen and learn. They have clearly changed her life. I have great admiration for her continued commitment to Maasai women and girls."

—Joseph Lewis, Ed.D

"As so often happens, people who set out to make a change in the world find that they not only made a difference in those they wanted to help, but these experiences end up cutting to the very core of their own hearts. The change that occurs inside them is equal, or surpasses their initial mission. This book reveals stories of desperate women with hidden strengths whose lives have touched the author as she relays details of the work she has accomplished, and informs us of the tasks that still need to be done. Her journey touches not only Tanzania, but echoes around the world to inspire everyone. My own heart sings her praises as she motivates us to join in her quest to help others."

—Connie Bickman, author of Tribe of Women

"*A Full Circle* tells of the remarkable relationships that develop out of Deb Pangerl's journey from Minnesota to Tanzania and the enriching exchange that takes place with the Maasai people. A Full Circle's map to a meaningful life journey doesn't require distant travel. It starts with an open heart, the vision to see beyond superficial barriers, and the courage to experience and respect the profound wonder of all human- ity. An enjoyable read for all sojourners."

—Kathleen A. Moccio

A
Full Circle

Walking alongside Maasai
Women of Tanzania

Debra Pangerl

BEAVER'S POND
PRESS

Many of the individuals and events described in this book are composites based on actual individuals and events. Some of the names and other characteristics have been changed to protect the identities of the persons described.

ISBN: 978-1-59298-446-6
Library of Congress Control Number: 2011942697

Printed in the United States of America
Cover photograph by Mary Bach
Book design by Ryan Scheife, Mayfly Design
First Printing: 2012

16 15 14 13 12   5 4 3 2 1

Beaver's Pond Press, Inc.
7104 Ohms Lane, Suite 101
Edina, MN 55439-2129
(952) 829-8818
www.BeaversPondPress.com
To order, visit www.BeaversPondBooks.com
or call (800) 901-3480. Reseller discounts available.

CONTENTS

"We [Maasai women] are a very backward people because we are not educated. . . . We are treated like a sack of corn that can be tossed about, this way and that. We are despised in general because we have no education. It makes me feel very low in my heart."

—A courageous Maasai woman

"I have heard of this thing called education. Do you think it will help my granddaughter?"

—A Maasai grandmother

*To all of the girls and women in the world
whose voices are heard in this book.*

GRATITUDE

When I started to write this page, I realized that over the past several years nearly everyone I talked to about this book helped me in some way, however small. They gave advice, offered their insight, or merely listened and supported my writing. I knew I could never name everyone. To everyone left unmentioned, my deepest apologies and gratitude for your help. Many times I changed a name or details to preserve someone's privacy. I apologize for any instance in which I have mistaken details or inadvertently caused pain. This book owes its life and merits to so many. Any errors or inadequacies that remain are my own.

To my family and friends who have been so supportive: I can't begin to express the words to thank all of you. I hope you know what a difference your presence has made in my life.

I am deeply grateful to Phoebe Msigomba, Richard Lubawa, and Tasiana Njau. Without you and so many others in Tanzania, there would be fewer relationships and changed lives on both sides of the ocean. Your compassion, commitment, and nonjudgmental ways, along with your friendship, are gifts that I deeply value.

Many thanks to those who spent many hours reading, editing, and proofing drafts of this book: Nancy Bussiere, Kelsie Brust, Jayne Pangerl, Gayla Marty, LaDez Pangerl, Amy Quale,

Gabrielle Mead, McKenzie Pangerl, Stacy Lynn Bettison, Ryan Scheife, and Jennifer Manion.

To my editor, Margaret Marty: I owe so much. You inspired me by your positive words, encouraged me when I needed it, and shared great wisdom when I hesitated.

Special thanks to Mary Bach who spent countless hours assisting me in emptying my heart onto these pages and helping me find the words to depict the meaning I wanted to convey.

Thanks to John Foley for taking precious time to give me encouragement and providing thoughtful edits to the manuscript.

I am forever grateful to my personal coaches who guided me along the right path during the writing of this book: Anita Janssen, Mike Foley, and Sherri Petersen. They had the right words at the right times to keep me on my path.

So many donors, volunteers, and valuable mentors of the IMAGE Project have inspired me—I could never name every one.

I feel a huge sense of privilege, honor, and humility knowing the courageous Maasai girls and women featured in this book. I have emptied onto these pages the difficult stories I have carried with me for so long. I hope to lift up the voices of my Maasai friends who so courageously have shared their stories with me and raised awareness that as women our aspirations, hopes, and dreams are far more alike than different. My thanks to all of the girls and women in all of the Maasai villages, especially the women in the village of Kwale: Merina, Monica, Helena, Eva, Leah, Pendo, Secilia, Magreth, Judith, Martha, Mariamu, Maria, Lusiana, Mary, Ana, Wema,

Esta, Merina, Kalayai, Magreti, Joice, Yese, Anita, Matibo, Lea, Rehema, and Mama R.—thank you from the bottom of my heart.

To my dear husband Gary . . . not a day goes by that I don't feel grateful that you are in my life and for your willingness to give yourself so that I could take time from our lives together to pursue my own purpose and write this book.

Most of all, I thank God for leading me on this extraordinary journey.

FOREWORD

Tanzania is a beautiful country of dramatic contrasts: riches and poverty, hope and despair. Surprisingly, her greatest assets are not the largest free-roaming herds of animals in the world; it is the Tanzanian people, whose deeply rooted culture so powerfully transcends the poverty they find themselves in.

When Minnesotan Debra Pangerl found herself teaching in Tanzania more than twenty years ago, she did not realize that the assignment would also be the first step in finding *herself*. Like most visitors to this mysterious and fascinating East African country, Pangerl was drawn to the Tanzanian people, particularly the women, but most especially the proud, but oppressed women of the Maasai tribe.

A Full Circle is a fitting title to Pangerl's deeply engaging book about her work among Maasai women and girls as she answers a strong inner call to return to Tanzania. She travels to a host of remote villages and does something many Western volunteers forget to do: she listens intently and asks the women and girls how she can help them. Having earned their trust, she and her colleagues in the IMAGE Project set out to educate the maasai girls and women who have asked their assistance in getting an education. In helping *them* find themselves, Pangerl comes to realize that they are helping her as much as she is helping them. She has in fact come full circle.

I recommend this book, not only for its narrative of how one nongovernmental organization importantly changes the lives of so many, but it is also a beautiful story of how unselfish giving also leads to powerful self-discovery.

Kjell Bergh, Consul (Hon.)
United Republic of Tanzania
Minneapolis, MN

INTRODUCTION

I started to write this book because I was filled with the heart-wrenching, inspiring stories that Maasai women and girls have shared with me over a span of ten years. Compelled to share their stories with others, I grappled with another issue stirring inside me as I wrote, ultimately finding the freedom to be content with who I am and what I have experienced in my life. I have learned that it is only in being true to ourselves that we can become who we were meant to be in this world.

God has taken my past, woven it into the lives of my Maasai friends who've experienced so much difficulty in their lives, and shown all of us that, by being authentic and trusting God, we can give ourselves permission to be who we were meant to be. Each of us can rise above our past and live for today—rather than bring the past into today, and let it become part of our future.

If I hadn't made mistakes and overcome challenges in my life—challenges that caused me to question who I was and what my life purpose was—I probably would never have returned to Tanzania after my initial trip in 1989. But because I was searching for answers, I did return. What I saw in the lives of the Maasai compelled me to be true to my purpose and do what I could to empower them to change their own lives.

It is clear to me that I am to speak for those who have no voice. There was a time, many years ago, when I felt as if I had no voice; today, I do, and it is with that voice and my compassion for the Maasai women that I have written this book.

My Journey

CHAPTER 1

The Seed is Planted

We are all born with exactly what we need to fulfill our purpose in the world.

—Anonymous

The meddling of my soul began early in 1989. I had just been to the gas station. I couldn't even afford to fill the tank, but I figured that if I put in five dollars, perhaps I could get to college and back for two days.

I was starting to feel like myself again, getting back on my feet after a painful divorce. I was emotionally drained, but knew that I could find my self-worth somewhere, if I put my attention to searching for it. To others, my life appeared complete, but I was putting the pieces of what seemed like a fragile life back together, and I found it difficult to see my path. Without any idea where I was going, I was taking one day at a time and pursuing my undergraduate degree so I could support myself. Other than that—anything was possible. I was truly going through the void, carefully feeling my way, open to a new future.

At my apartment, I picked up the travel section of the Minneapolis *Star Tribune*. Boom! It hit me! The words jumped off the paper: "Volunteers needed to go to Tanzania, Africa."

The appeal was made by an organization called Global Volunteers, a private, nonprofit, nonsectarian, nongovernmental organization engaging short-term volunteers to work on micro-economic and human development programs in close partnership with local people worldwide. I felt a pull so strong that I can only refer to it as a calling from deep within my soul.

I had no money, nor did I know a way of getting any. Besides, I was in college, and so was not a good candidate for traveling abroad outside the context of school. Although these rationalizations made sense, I felt deep within me that I *had* to go. There was something about the appeal that I had read in the paper that grabbed me and wouldn't let go.

I began telling people that I was going—I was not sure how, but it didn't matter. I must admit, I was somewhat apprehensive of going by myself, so I asked my Aunt Franny if she would allow my cousin Ann, a junior in high school, to come along. Ann was thrilled. We began making plans.

In November, we boarded a plane for Tanzania. By then, we had raised enough money for airfare by having bake sales, speaking about the trip to local organizations, and taking a loan for the balance from Aunt Franny. Everything we needed was stuffed into army duffle bags and away we went. Our mission as part of Global Volunteers was simple: promote international peace. I could do that. Or at least I could try.

Arriving at our base in Iringa, Tanzania, we were reminded that the Lutheran church would be our host.

"Remember three things," cautioned our host. "The bugs are your friends, don't go near the army camp, and always stay in pairs."

It sounded simple. I felt qualified, even though I had never traveled outside of the United States. I resolved to follow the rules and felt certain all would be fine. The motto of our group was, *Expect the unexpected and receive it calmly, with good humor.* I would soon find out the necessity of this simple phrase.

We left Iringa for the village of Pommern. Two hours by vehicle took us through red clay roads with potholes so large I could stand in them. Throughout the ride, we sat on blow-up donut cushions because the seats were made of unpadded boards. The scenery was breathtaking—green and lush—reminiscent of scenes from the movie *Out of Africa.*

Our home for the next three weeks was an old mission house, a two-story, all-brick building that the Germans had built during World War II. There was no running water or indoor plumbing, and most of the cooking was done outside over a pit in the ground. The Germans had left some barracks, and our job, beginning the next morning, was to renovate them into classrooms for secondary students.

We awakened to the voices of children singing as they walked by our open windows on their way to school. Accompanying the beautiful sound was the scent of eucalyptus drifting through the air.

As the days of this relatively short visit went by, I couldn't help but observe how many Tanzanians went through their lives without many material things, things that most Americans, myself included, considered indispensible. We generally took so much for granted, including running water, electricity, and cupboards filled with food. Even as I saw what was lacking, I discovered how simple and beautiful the Tanzanians' lives were. Later I would learn about their struggles to survive. But on this first visit, they seemed supremely happy, despite what I saw was missing from their lives. How could that be?

I found myself settling in and sleeping more comfortably after someone loaned me a little *paka* (the Swahili word for kitten) as my bedtime companion. The kitten was actually there to help manage rats, which I found terrifying. This was Africa, and the experience was already opening my eyes to the immense differences in how people live around the world.

For three weeks, our six members taught English to students at the secondary school while we also renovated classrooms. Phoebe, a middle-aged woman, was an excellent interpreter, and we learned much about Tanzania from her. I had no idea at that time how meaningful my relationship with Phoebe would become.

The end of the trip came too soon. A strange feeling swept over me as we said goodbye to our new friends, to our interpreter Phoebe, and our driver Simon, assuming I would never return to Africa in my lifetime. We'd heard rumors that the Lutheran church in Tanzania might be working with the Lutheran church in America. Because I had been raised Catholic, I didn't have any idea that this could be significant to me. All I did was promise to write to Phoebe. Without my awareness, what I experienced and saw in those villages was taking root and would grow as time went on.

Returning to my apartment in Minneapolis, I fell back into my normal life. Sitting at the kitchen table, staring out the window at the freshly fallen snow, I struggled to write a college paper about Africa for my sociology class. I had initially believed that I made that trip to Africa to change something about their culture, so they could be more like us. But it was dawning on me that I wanted what they had: the peace and contentment evident in their lives.

Perhaps I needed a fresh look at my own life. I had been searching for peace since I had made a decision to leave a broken marriage. Yet I continued to ask myself questions about the choices I had made and God's plan for my life

Something was missing, and at that point, I didn't have a clue what that might be.

CHAPTER 2

The Journey Continues

Be still and know that I am God.

—Psalm 46:10

I began dating Gary, my husband-to-be, in 1991, just at the time I was filling out a Peace Corps application, still trying to find answers about what my Tanzanian friends had in Africa that I didn't have in America. But I knew my place was with Gary—not with the Peace Corps. As we discussed our plans for the future, Gary was curious about Africa. I had already shared with him the deep impact that trip made on me.

He asked, "Do you think you will ever go back to Africa?"

I told him the possibility was slim.

Gary and I were married in 1993. The next year, we moved to the small town where he had grown up. Life was simple and complete. I had a loving husband who was my best friend. I had a great job that I loved, along with everything else anyone could want. Yet my soul still yearned for something, and I couldn't solve the mystery. *What was it? Where could I find it?* Although I didn't realize it at the time, the seeds sown during my earlier experience in Africa had taken root within me and something new was growing.

Maybe I was looking for a deeper meaning. Maybe I was looking for my life's purpose.

All of this was new to me. I found myself drawn to books about caring for my soul and finding purpose. I also began trying to make my life simpler by imitating what I had seen in Africa, in people with far fewer material goods who lived richer lives.

Finally, I attended a retreat. There, I experienced a deep spiritual awakening. On a particular day that is recorded in my heart, I found the meaning and direction for which I had been searching. On November 23, 1998, I saw *the sun rise— when the sun had already set for the day* on a snowy evening in Little Falls, Minnesota. When I shared this revelation with the resident pastor at the retreat, he said, "The Son has indeed risen in your heart." My faith journey had begun.

The next summer, I attended an evening service at First Lutheran Church in Rush City, a church that Gary and I had joined. Pastor Sue Tjornehoj, an inspiring visiting pastor, spoke about the St. Paul-Area Synod having a companion congregation in Tanzania, very close to the area I had visited in 1989. I could barely sit still in my pew, although at the time I told myself it was just a coincidence.

Pastor Tjornehoj invited me to attend a fall gathering to meet with others interested in helping with the work in Tanzania. While there, she asked if I would be interested in becoming a member of the St. Paul-Area Synod Task Force with Tanzania. I was thrilled, to say the least. Somehow, I knew this was no coincidence. I was blessed to be presented with an opportunity that truly aligned with who I had become following my first trip. I accepted immediately.

But I also knew I needed to fess up to Gary that very night. I said, "Gary, I'm getting that feeling again about going to Africa." At first, I think he didn't believe I was serious, since he just smiled. But later, looking back, I realized that maybe he hadn't been so surprised after all.

Soon I began working on our church's companion congregation program for a small village called Kitowo, very close to Pommern in Tanzania. We supported village projects and also sponsored students in secondary school. I knew that the time I'd spent being still and listening for direction from within had led me to this moment.

CHAPTER 3

East-African Women's Issues

Your vision will become clear only when
you can look into your own heart.

—Carl Jung

Pastor Sue Tjornehoj called me unexpectedly in early 2000 to tell me that she had recommended me to study women's issues in East Africa in the fall with a group of twenty-five women from the United States and ten from Malawi, Kenya, Ethiopia, and Tanzania. The trip was organized by WELCA (Women of the Evangelical Lutheran Church of America) and Global Mission. To participate, I had to agree to volunteer as a global advocate. I didn't know what form the advocacy would take, but I decided to apply and was accepted. The two-year commitment seemed to fit into my life at the time. Of course, I didn't accept until after I told Gary that the calling was clear once again. Once again, he just smiled. He fully supported my choices. I was fortunate, unlike many of the women I had already met on my journey.

I left for East Africa in November 2000. My seventy-six-year-old mother, a close family friend, and two other women from our church also left around the same time to work with our companion congregation. I met them in Iringa after my two-week study seminar in Kenya and northern Tanzania ended.

When we arrived in Kenya, we met the other women from East Africa who were chosen to represent their respective countries and churches. The representative from Tanzania was Phoebe Msigomba, whom I had met in 1989! Our paths had crossed again.

Our women's study group started out from Nairobi, Kenya's capital. Only one day into our trip, I realized that I had never seen such severe poverty. A drought was affecting the country at the time, and the scenes pierced my heart and turned my stomach. Buildings looked like they were in scenes from a war movie. The clusters of people we passed looked hopeless and appeared to be walking aimlessly. Beggars pleaded for help from other locals who themselves had nothing to give. I asked myself, *How can I exist in this world and not reach out to them?* I had so much. I was so content with my life, yet the person I was becoming somehow found this contentment unsettling. How would I ever be able to go home and continue with my life as if this part of the world didn't exist?

As part of our work together, the group visited the Mwangaza Partnership in Arusha, where women were empowered by receiving educations, giving them newfound confidence and sense of self. The Mwangaza Partnership is a grassroots, faith-based organization that fosters a variety of learning programs. Surprisingly, this visit provided me with a lesson I needed to learn: how to say no and set boundaries before I found myself in situations in which I didn't intend to become involved.

During a tour of the facility, one of the women made a simple but profound statement: "In the light of God, we are all one color." For all of us in the study group, this expression of unity reaffirmed our desire to work with and learn from each other.

Another woman said, "When my husband leaves for a cool beer, I leave for a seminar at the Mwangaza Partnership." I could sense how much the exposure to education had empowered her. I was inspired and felt a growing determination to do more.

The next morning we visited the Maasai Girls Lutheran Secondary School near Arusha. The school and programs were very impressive, and I found myself in awe of the girls. They had a hunger in their eyes—not for food, but for education. They crowded close to me as they asked questions about where I lived, what I did, and what my country was like. They were so curious about everything in the world. I felt the power of their hunger.

We learned that many of the Maasai girls did not go home during break; if they did, their parents would immediately marry them off to older men.

Phoebe told me that Maasai people lived where she lived in Iringa. I found that interesting, as I had been there before, but hadn't heard much about the Maasai at that time. I was intrigued.

Phoebe and I continued our discussion of the Maasai girls over the next few days. She thought perhaps we could work together on a way to help the girls in the Iringa area. I knew it was possible; I just didn't know what to do next. We kept talking it over as we continued on our journey. Phoebe told me the Tanzanian government only pays for children to attend school through seventh grade. After that, it is the parent's responsibility to pay for the children to attend secondary school. Tanzania is the fourth poorest country in the world, with an average yearly salary of $300. Tuition at a private school costs $350 per year, leaving little chance for girls to even dream of going to school.

Each evening during the trip, different women from East Africa gave presentations on the issues confronting women in their countries. Every story touched me deeply.

One woman named Sara said, "So many people in my community are ignorant. They do not know technology, and they are living below the poverty level. It is these women who suffer the most. We are hoping to create a platform for discussion on change, and our goals are: feed the hungry, refresh the thirsty, welcome the strangers, clothe the naked, and care for the prisoners."

Another woman, Elizabeth, discussed female genital mutilation. I didn't know much about this practice at the time and was shocked when I heard the stories.

Elizabeth said, "Many people in my community believe that if a young girl fails to have this done to her, she will become sick and will never marry. Men say to us, 'Women are inferior.' Why are the men the decision makers? Why can't we make decisions?"

I had no reply. I sat before her, stunned. Then the conversation shifted to infant dumping. "Sometimes we have to throw the infants into dustbins or into the jungle if they are born with disabilities or if we can't afford to keep them," Elizabeth added, tears glistening in her eyes. "Sometimes we really want to keep them, but other women tell us to accept this practice as a way of survival."

She continued, "Girls are supposed to be *good girls.* If they get pregnant while unmarried, the boys are never mentioned. A boy may threaten to kill a girl if she should ever mention she was raped. The older men want the younger girls, believing they are safe from AIDS, but now those same so-called *safe girls* have contracted AIDS from the older men.

"This life continues and the women and girls suffer silently," Elizabeth concluded.

A third woman named Deborah said, "The woman is the last person to sleep and the first to get up in the morning, because there is so much manual labor to be done. Women visit the poor and bring them sugar or anything to cheer them up."

She asked us, "How do you shape your children?" *Yes, how do we?* I thought. It was a great question.

The presentation of Abera, an Ethiopian woman, remains imprinted in my mind after all these years. I can still see her strength and conviction as she spoke. Abera began her turn by talking about female genital mutilation, which was becoming a major theme in all presentations. We wanted to learn more, although what we heard disturbed us.

"At age seven, the clitoris is cut from young girls," Abera explained. "They are kidnapped in order to have this done. Then the vagina is sewn shut to protect the girls from aggressive men.

"On the night of their marriage, if the husband can't break through into the vagina, he may have a friend help him," she continued. "Later, if the husband goes away from the home for any period of time, the vagina is sewn shut again, so his wife can't have sex with anyone while he is away. Ninety percent of Ethiopian women are circumcised."

Abera also talked about early marriages. "Girls are given up for marriage at the age of eight or nine," she said. "A boy is told he can marry her and he is allowed to have sexual intercourse with her at this early age. Some girls become pregnant as early as twelve years, but they are not yet fully developed physically. Therefore, they have to push so hard to deliver the baby that the mother's internal organs are damaged. Then infection sets in and the wound begins to smell. So the boy gives her back to her family to live in hardship and poverty.

"In some areas of Ethiopia, if the hands of a baby are first to come out of the mother in the birthing process, the baby is considered born under a curse," she continued. "The mother must throw the baby into a pit. If she won't do so, the tribe takes the baby by force.

"Few women in Ethiopia are educated," she went on to say. "They are considered property of the men. A husband can use a woman to have sex, and throw her back to her family when he is done with her. When a man is asked how many children he has, he lists only the boys, not the girls. A female is not counted as an individual in our culture."

Hearing such stories was overwhelming. I had trouble comprehending how this reality could so invisibly exist in our modern world. How could this be? Then I realized it was because many East African women and girls had never had a voice before. No one had listened to their stories.

One other woman spoke up. She asked us, "Why have only men been coming to our countries? For years we have wondered, 'Where are the women? Why aren't they coming?' We have been waiting to tell our stories."

The Boys Street Project
We also visited the Boys Street Project in Nairobi. Its purpose is to save young children from poverty by going onto the streets of Nairobi at six in the morning to collect street chil-

dren and bring them to their center. The center's workers do this in the early morning because the homeless children are easy to spot. Children who have parents who are still able to care for them are at their homes asleep at that hour. Some of the street children have left their homes as young as age five because of the severe poverty caused by the area's drought. They and their parents know that the children have a better chance of finding food and water on the streets than in their homes, even at age five.

At the end of the day I was at a loss. I was exhausted from the despair. I could only pray, *God, I have heard your children cry. How do I help?* I had never seen or heard so much suffering. I knew I couldn't process any more—my heart and mind were full. So many people were overflowing with pain and suffering, yet at the same time, their strength and humility touched me deeply. I wondered how they endured. Some time later I received my answer; a woman said to me, "We cry in the morning, so we can laugh in the afternoon."

Refuse Company

The next day we visited a women-run refuse company. As I prepared for the visit, I figured that there I would have relief from the suffering I had been witnessing, because we were simply going to learn about garbage processing in Kenya. I was wrong.

The owner had started the garbage company in 1992 with the goal of cleaning up the slums. As I heard her story, again I could feel my heart ache as she told us how they had found children playing in industrial waste when they entered the slums in Nairobi. Families were living in drastic conditions.

Mothers were mixing flour with the waste to feed their children since there was no food. Some garbage dumps, she told us, even contained remains of the deceased.

"As an individual," the owner stated, "I had to do something about what I was seeing. I decided to start a social service company within my garbage company to help the children we were finding." As she told me how she struggled to help them, I struggled to process all the haunting things I had seen thus far.

Kenya AIDS Clinic
The following day, we visited an AIDS clinic in Nairobi. The clinic provided counseling and group therapy to women with AIDS, and we were able to hear the stories of some of these remarkable women.

Mimi was from the slums. She had been diagnosed with AIDS in 1992. She had five children and one grandchild. She was living on the street for two months prior to our visit because she had no money.

Anwanga had four children and no one to care for them. She was sick all the time, but her neighbors had too many of their own problems and couldn't help her. Weeping, she said, "If you have seen a mother suffering, you have seen how the whole family lives."

Mary lived in the slums. She collected used maize (corn) from the garbage, mixed it with flour, and cooked it for her children. She told us the stigma of having AIDS is great.

They asked us, "Do you have HIV-positive people in your country? How do you help them?" It was a simple question, but one we could not answer easily.

During our visit, one woman received vitamins from the clinic staff. As the afternoon went on and she lingered at the clinic, we observed that she held on to them tightly. We learned that she planned to take them home for her children, rather than use them for herself. We also learned that the clinic staff had no medicines to give to the women who came to see them, only vitamins. This was the desperate state of the clinic in an area in which one out of six people had AIDS.

Although unable to provide their clients with the medicines they needed, the clinic staff focused on building relationships, listening to their stories, crying with them, and helping them solve problems as best they can. One of the staff members helped them write memory books. They'd write about their favorite day, what their children loved, why they are sick, and at the end, they'd write about AIDS and how it changed their lives forever.

Mary's Story

Mary, a Maasai mother of three girls, told her story one evening at dusk. She recalled how her own mother often wondered how they would survive, as they had nothing, yet she was always saying, "The Lord will provide." Mary gave credit for her education to God. She was fortunate to have studied abroad in Dublin through a missionary program. The education she received changed the path of her life.

"Most Maasai women till the land by hand, prepare food for the home, and walk—sometimes a full day—to fetch water from a river," Mary said. "Maasai women cannot own anything. They are treated like pieces of property." The injustice of this became apparent to her when she pursued her education abroad.

She spoke with conviction as she continued, "Education is very, very important to Maasai girls and women. Maasai women need to know their rights and their value as human beings. They need to learn how to stand up and say no to the harsh treatment they endure as women."

Traditions, however, die hard, something that Mary and women of her community witnessed on a daily basis. The only way out of these traditions, Mary knew, was through learning. Education is a golden chance for a young girl.

"If they don't go to school," Mary went on, "they are exposed to circumcision at an early age, often causing death. Marriages are arranged as early as twelve to fourteen years of age. Many times the scar from the circumcision ruptures during childbirth, causing the mother to bleed to death. Early marriages also cause infertility because of immature bodies having to deliver babies. Some women pretend to be sick all the time just to keep their old husbands away."

After Mary had been to secondary school for three years, her father decided she'd had enough education. But her mother was a brave woman. She stepped in with courage and said, "If Mary doesn't finish school, she will become the third or fourth wife to an old man. I want a better life for my daughter."

The Kibera Slums of Nairobi
On a later day, we arrived in the slums of Nairobi in the early morning. My fellow passengers on the bus and I became increasingly silent as we moved through the streets. Noth-

ing could have prepared us for the sights we saw. I couldn't imagine how anything could be worse—we saw nothing but garbage, dirt, and waste. There was little space in which to walk, yet the neighborhoods were densely populated with very young, tiny children and their caregivers. I saw hollow eyes on all the children, as well as the adults—perhaps from hunger, perhaps from the depths of despair.

Our group remained silent during our visit, which lasted half a day. I am sure the others were similarly shocked by what they saw, given the living conditions we all witnessed. Anxiety rose in me as I sat on the bus preparing to depart, and I felt a very unfamiliar and dark energy.

Upon leaving the slums, my eyes captured sight of a little boy in ragged clothing carrying his younger sister on his back. He appeared to be around five years old—just like the little children I had learned about previously, children who leave their homes to try to exist on the street. *Perhaps he is one of those*, I thought.

In the next instant, our eyes locked, and his look alone seemed to say, *Please help me*. I couldn't. The bus I was on just kept driving through the slums. And I suddenly became overwhelmed as tears filled my eyes. I wept for the children who have to leave their homes at the mere age of five to go out into the streets, who carry their siblings on their backs; for the mothers who had nothing to feed their children; for the many people forced to live in darkness; and for their hopelessness.

I couldn't take it in—I felt numb, like there was nothing left of me. My energy had been drained by the sights I had seen. *Who was that little boy?* I kept thinking. To me he represented the dark new world so recently revealed to me.

Reflections

At the end of our journey with the women of East Africa, our team leaders asked us to reflect on the African women who had stood before us and told their stories—women who had spoken from the depths of their hearts and who gave voice to their experiences and lives. We now knew of their struggles. The African women had shed tears as they told their stories, tears they described as *agents of healing*.

Later that evening, a woman from East Africa boldly said, "It's sometimes scary to put our lives in the hands of the Holy Spirit, because it may take us places we don't want to go." Her words really spoke to me.

Our team leaders suggested we ask ourselves some questions: How did the experiences that we had shared together make us better people? Where would this experience take us in our lives? Would we go willingly? They told us to recall the words of Jesus from Luke 12:48: *From everyone who has been given much, much will be demanded; and from the one who has been entrusted with much, much more will be asked.* They reminded us that God had a plan for each one of us, if we let Him use our lives. When they posed these questions to us, I knew I would need time to answer them. We had learned so much.

At the end of the trip, Phoebe and I left one another, not knowing whether our futures would bring us geographically together again. Yet it was clear we would somehow work together to make a difference in the world. We had seen so much and our hearts were inspired to take action. We had to help in some way. I knew full well that the eyes of the little boy I had seen while I had been riding the bus would haunt me day and night if I didn't do something more.

CHAPTER 4

Sharing What I Witnessed

*God calls you to the place where your deep gladness
and the world's deep hunger meet.*

—Frederick Buechner

Early in 2001, I shared stories from my 2000 trip to East
Africa at Our Redeemer Lutheran Church in Pine City, Minnesota. It was my first presentation as a global advocate. A few
days before, I'd received a letter from Phoebe telling me that
four little Maasai girls were at her home in Tanzania. Their
mothers had brought them hundreds of miles in the back of
dump trucks so they could have a chance to receive an education. I wrote back to Phoebe that I would try to raise some
funds to help the girls, but I could give her no guarantee.

I spoke to a small group of women at the church that Saturday, many of whom were on fixed incomes. My mind still
struggled to fully absorb the stories I had heard, stories that
had tried to recede into my subconscious because they were
so painful to recall, but despite my difficulty, I was able to tell
them some of the incredible stories I had heard.

The group of women in Pine City passed a handmade African basket around after I spoke. I was stunned at their generosity. They had placed nearly $1,400 in the basket. This was enough to keep all four girls in school for one full year. I was humbled again by the power of these stories to move not only me, but other women who had only glimpsed the experiences of African women through my words.

Around the same time, three women from Tanzania came to Minnesota to speak at the Global Mission Conference in Minneapolis. Two of them were women I had met on my 2000 Africa trip. I offered Mary and Elizabeth, both Maasai women, and Judith, a Tanzanian woman who worked with HIV/AIDS orphans, a place to stay in our home.

As I drove the women to my house, I apologized in advance for all the *stuff* I owned—ten pairs of shoes on the back of the spare bedroom door, multiple televisions, and dressers of extra clothing. It was a house filled with *stuff*. I was embarrassed by how sharply it contrasted with what they—and countless other women—had in Tanzania.

"Don't worry about how much you have, as long as you share it," Judith volunteered. She was amazed, she told me, that in the United States we get to decide what we want to eat when we order from restaurant menus. In her country at mealtime, women must decide which child goes without. Her small, unassuming remark left me with a feeling that I had to do more.

During their stay with us, I took the women to visit our local small-town grocery store. As we slowly moved through the aisles, Mary called out, "Judith, come and look! This whole store is filled with food!" My neighbors in the store stared humbly at the floor as they came to understand that in the United States, we have so much, while in other countries, there is so little.

In March, 2002, I wrote an article on Tanzania for *Lutheran Woman Today* magazine. At the last minute, I decided, on my own, to include a short note at the end: If you would like to make a contribution to help sponsor the Maasai girls, please send it to . . ." To my surprise, funds started pouring in from women across the United States. It was evident that American women cared about the African girls and women who suffered the plights that I had seen and written about. They wanted to help with their education.

I was astonished, but so glad, that this problem had solved itself. I had been lying awake at night worrying, thinking, *How will I pay for the education costs for the additional new girls that are arriving and depending on me? What if the money doesn't come in?* I still had doubts that I would be able to finish what I'd started. Yet at the same time, I was beginning to realize that God was using me to work with others to provide for the needs of these girls and women.

Before long I had to tell Gary for the third time that I felt "the calling" to go back to Tanzania. I was grateful that I had married someone who supported me as I made my way on this journey. This time, I went with our own church group to visit our companion congregation, and I visited with the girls who were taking presecondary classes at Phoebe's home.

It was during this trip in 2004 that Phoebe came up with the idea of calling our work "the IMAGE Project." The name reflected the fact that we are all made in the image of God. The name also stood for "Iringa MAasai Girls Education."

CHAPTER 5

Confirming the Needs of the Maasai

Whatever you are meant to do, move
toward it and it will come to you.

—Gloria Dunn

In 2006, I knew I had to return to Tanzania. My goal was to find out if education was a priority that the Maasai genuinely wanted for their future. I planned to accomplish this by spending time conversing with them in their villages.

My focus on the trip was to listen and learn. I did not wish to push anything on the people I would meet, nor did I want to change their culture. It was not my goal to "rescue" them, but instead to work with them to improve their lives in the direction they chose.

Phoebe had taken a fulltime teaching position, so Dr. Richard Lubawa, a Tanzanian man who dedicated his life to helping people in his country, began working with me because of his interest in the Maasai. Phoebe and Richard both previously worked at the Iringa Diocese together.

Because of Richard's deep relationship with the Maasai, we were welcomed into the villages. His kind spirit and compassion for the girls and women allowed our relationship with the Maasai to flourish. Richard and his wife, Dorothy, have taken many thirteen- to seventeen-year-old girls into their homes under the cover of night. The girls were looking for an opportunity to attend secondary school.

During this trip, Richard took us to three Maasai villages that he had previously visited. At the first village, the chief greeted us. His eyes twinkled as he smiled and said, "I have heard that you were coming, but my eyes never thought they would ever see you. I think I am dreaming."

We drove our vehicle to a corral made of thorn bushes and sticks; then we were shown to an area under a tree where we could sit down. We decided to show them personal family photograph albums we had brought along. The women and children huddled around us to see, and I was nearly buried by their bodies. I began speaking about the photos in English, forgetting they did not understand, but they responded by saying, "Uhhh huhhh . . . uhhh huhhhh," and nodding their heads.

Communicating without truly speaking—that's what we were doing. It felt like an old-fashioned Sunday afternoon in Minnesota, sitting under the tree, visiting with friends and family. It was so peaceful. I realized how much Maasai women had already enriched my life, and I was beginning to understand how different, yet similar, our lives were.

Next, the Maasai girls who were benefitting from our new program stood in front of us with their families, looking beautiful in their silver jewelry and bright-blue dresses. That day, we were fortunate to be able to take many photographs, which captured the girls' beauty. They were now attending secondary school in a nearby village. We asked their families if things were more difficult in the village, now that many of their daughters were attending secondary school a long distance from their homes.

A man answered, "Maybe sometimes the girls could be herding goats or something, but you could not compare that with giving a girl an education."

This was the first time I had heard from a Maasai man that education was something of value in the life of a girl. I was beginning to find the answer to the question I came with, namely: Did the Maasai feel that it was important for girls to get an education?

At the end of our visit, a father stood up proudly. He was a strong Maasai warrior, and he spoke with eloquence. "In our Swahili language, we have the word *asante*, which means thank you. Even if we continue saying the word forty times, the word will keep on coming. So when we use the word over and over, it is because we lack another word to thank you for coming to help our daughters. We pray God will keep on blessing you, so that you can continue doing the same for other daughters and continue with the same spirit."

From this village, we continued on our journey. Branches hit the side of our vehicle as we followed the narrow cow path through the thorny bush to our next stop. As we approached, I was excited to see the village was very small—only a few huts—and I happily thought that our visit would be very intimate. As soon as we arrived, I noticed a small goat being led away behind the hut. *That's interesting*, I remember thinking. *I didn't know that the Maasai lead goats around.* I found out later that it became our lunch.

The members of the village enjoyed our photographs, and we felt warmly welcomed. Then we started talking about education. Their first question was "Why are you helping us?" I had anticipated that eventually someone would ask that question. After all, wouldn't we wonder the same thing, if someone volunteered to help us?

While the village women sat on dried cowhide feeding their babies milk from long, golden, gourd-type bottles decorated with colored beads, I told them about the little boy I had seen in Nairobi and how I wanted to do my part in the world. I told them that we were making possible educational opportunities for over thirty Maasai girls in their area, and I wanted to learn about the many challenges that Massai women faced trying to educate their children.

As they sat intently listening, I explained why I had come halfway around the world to help their daughters. I told them how the IMAGE Project had changed the direction and focus of my life and how God was somehow weaving our lives together. I began by telling them about some events that had changed my life, including what had happened after my father's death.

"In 1989, Dad's health began to fail from a terminal heart condition," I told them. "He was a man of tremendous faith, and I wanted to find some peace dealing with his death. I had to search deep within my heart to find the peace I so desperately wanted. My dad's death taught me how to live, and I felt God's grace like never before, filling me with peace. To me, part of Dad's reason for living was dying. He taught me so much about life.

"Then I was on a business trip with a friend, John Lee. As we walked off the plane in California, John complained of a headache. In a matter of seconds, he was sweating profusely, so I tried to help him remove his suit coat. He was mumbling words, but I was unable to understand what he was trying to say. Sitting in a chair, he suddenly began having seizures, and slid onto the floor. I tried again to help him get his jacket off, but I couldn't. Just as I touched him again, I felt something I had never felt before, and then the feeling was gone. It was big and full one moment, and in an instant, it was gone.

"I rode in the ambulance with John after the paramedics arrived. I knew they were trying to revive him, and the horror of what was happening was too great for me to comprehend. We had just been going to work. I prayed every prayer I knew as the ambulance screamed to the hospital—the same hospital where we were to be working that morning. Upon arrival, he was taken in for brain surgery.

"When the surgeons came out after only an hour, I knew it was too soon for the surgery to be finished. John had a malignant tumor on his brain and the doctors could not save him. Although he was never aware of it, a tumor had been doubling in size every thirty days for quite some time. The doctor said, 'John must have been a great man, because he has been spared what would have been difficult days ahead with this tumor.' I could only nod my head in agreement.

"John had been fifty-nine years old, a picture of health. He had no idea he would die that day. I'm telling you this story because I could not have dealt with this experience in the same way before my faith was strengthened. Yes, God and I even had some disagreements over this situation; in fact, I was mad at God for a while. I thought that He should have sent someone else to be with John that day, someone who could have been of better help.

"I had wanted to save John, but it hadn't been possible. But we weren't alone that day. God had been with us, and I had felt his presence. One minute John was alive, and in the next few minutes, I saw him dying. As the pastor at the hospital said, 'Death comes to us like a thief in the night—you never know when it's coming, so you always need to be ready.'

"My life was changing. Death was teaching me valuable lessons. I was afraid of what could happen to me. Was I ready to meet God and tell him what I had done with the life he had given me? Was I really ready? What had I done with my life? Would it be enough to stand before God, the powerful and almighty, who I now believed really existed, and say I actually did something worthwhile with my life?

"I began to grow spiritually. I learned to trust God. On April 23, 2000, three months to the day of my father's death, I told God he could take my life and use it for whatever He had planned for me, and I would follow. Was I scared? Of course; but I knew there was more to life.

"That is the moment when big things began to happen in my life, and they have yet to stop. I have learned there are no coincidences. God has a plan for each of us. Every event or situation that happens is part of God's plan for our lives. I believe that God has led me to be with you today."

They were moved by my story and tears welled in the eyes of some. I felt connected to them in a way I couldn't explain. We continued our discussions about education for the Maasai girls, and later, my traveling companions and I continued by vehicle to the next village.

Our last stop on this trip was a small village near the river. Once again we were led to an area under a large acacia tree that was creaking in the wind. The day was becoming very hot.

The chief of this village sat in front of the women in his green short-sleeved American shirt, his colorful skirt wrapped up and around his knees. He began the conversation by saying, "Maasai women are like trophies. Once you get them, you put them somewhere. If they have no education, their rights pass them by."

Then an older chief of the same village who was sitting by another tree further away from us, spoke up. "When I die, I know that my children will have a better life with education."

We asked why some men still force their daughters to get married rather than to attend secondary school. "One man can have two thousand cows," the chief said, "yet he will still force a girl to get married because he doesn't want the child to lose her tradition. My father was laughed at because he wanted to send his son to school. Now it is coming to be the trend that younger boys are educated." It was encouraging to hear that the chief was supportive of traditions changing. Up until that time, a Maasai man might educate his son, but hardly ever a daughter.

"Why do you want to help us?" he asked.

"I had been listening to God and told Him that He could take my life and use it," I said. "When I stepped back and listened to God, He led me here, across the ocean. Whatever I learn from you gives my life meaning and purpose."

Just then a woman in the back row stood up tall and straight. Her voice was strong as she said with conviction, "We are a very backward people because we are not educated. We are despised at the hospital. We are treated like a sack of corn that can be tossed about, this way and that. We are despised in general because we have no education. It makes me feel very low in my heart."

It was so moving to hear them say these humble and difficult things. They were honest and outspoken about their experiences. We admired their boldness as we listened atten-tively. Their words and stories were making me delve deeper into myself to hone my own purpose and to determine how it was coinciding with their needs.

CHAPTER 6

Liaison in Tanzania

Our deepest fear is not that we are inadequate.
Our deepest fear is that we are powerful beyond measure.
It is our light, not our darkness that most frightens us.

—Marianne Williamson

When I returned to Minnesota from this trip, I felt very confident that educating girls was important to the Maasai. The idea was new to them, but they were generally supportive—both men and women. Now I wondered what to do with my new information. Since I worked at Dorsey & Whitney, a Minnesota law firm, I decided to investigate with our lawyers to see if they could help me start a nonprofit organization.

At the same time, I connected with my friend Anita Janssen, who was in the process of becoming certified in a life-coaching program. She was looking for someone with whom she could practice her coaching skills, prior to certification. Over the next two or three years, Anita worked with me (without charging me), coaching me on how to deal with the struggles and doubts I was experiencing, the decisions I needed to make about the organization, and the peace I needed to find.

We talked about how journaling can be healing, being versus doing, leading versus coordinating, finding one's purpose, dealing with different worldviews, thinking outside the box, finding balance in life, enjoying the journey, showing up differently, needing time for contemplation, and creating space for big things to happen. She also helped me address questions such as, *What is fact and what is story? What if I fail? What if I'm not good enough?*

Around this time, on September 6, 2007, I was sitting on the deck of our home. I had been working on finding my life's purpose, and it was proving to be a long process. The day was peaceful—sunny and gorgeous. A quote jumped out at me from the book I was reading:

If your purpose is aligned with the rest of the world, God will use you."

Another quote jumped out, this one by Albert Schweitzer:

At the point in your life when your talent meets the needs of the world, that is where God wants you to be."

I began writing the words that were coming to me: connect, Maasai, Africa, Tanzania, women, girls. Then I circled the ones that really compelled me. When I put the phrase "speak for those who have no voice" together, I felt an overpowering sense of peace within me. I knew I had my purpose—it felt rock hard, and still hasn't wavered. I knew who I was born to be and what I was meant to do.

During the time Anita was coaching me, the IMAGE

Project made tangible strides. Strategic planning resulted in the recruitment of board members, the creation of a website, the design of a brochure, and the development of presentation materials.

Liaison in East Africa

During this same time, Richard Lubawa began meeting with the Maasai elders in Tanzania. They told him that their government was asking them to reduce their herds of cattle and apply for licenses, so the government would know where they were living as semi-nomadic people. The elders were thinking of small projects for which the IMAGE Project could be of help, and the women were also thinking of ways we could work with them.

One day, Richard called me in Minnesota. "The women are interested in growing some crops," he said. "Would the IMAGE Project support this?"

"Absolutely!" I replied.

As this new project developed, with Richard as the leader, the women started working together in groups of four to six per plot. They learned how to grow sour tomatoes, corn, onions, and many types of beans. The first photos I received of the crop project showed the produce growing in an unorganized patch—no rows. As time went by, the gardens began to look like university demonstration plots, with all the plants lined up and the rows free of weeds.

Around the same time we were fortunate that a young woman named Tasiana joined the IMAGE Project as our coordinator. She had been working on her undergraduate degree at Tumaini University in Iringa. Even up until that time, Tasania had led an inspiring life that had brought her to deeply connect and appreciate the struggles of the Maasai women. As a reward for her stellar grades in high school, she had participated in field trips to the Maasai land near Arusha, Tanzania. There, she saw the poverty of the Maasai people, and knew in her heart that someday she would try to help them have better lives. Her applied intellect, openness, and compassion quickly made us realize how fortunate we were to have her working with us.

Clearly, transformation was upon all of us and many lives were being impacted positively through our efforts and the support of many other people. A long-time supporter Teresa Hasbrook, commented that her life had become richer because of her personal connection with the girls and women of the IMAGE Project. Even our contributors felt stirrings in their souls because of the courage and determination they heard about and saw in the stories and lives of the Maasai girls and women.

CHAPTER 7

The Women of Kwale Village

One gets outside the box by pushing
and stretching beyond ordinary limits.

—Anonymous

One of the villages that benefitted from our efforts in 2006 was the very small but progressive village of Kwale. Kwale is close to the great Ruaha River, which makes the area fertile for grazing. When we met and began working with them in 2006, the men and women of the village were forward thinking and willing to try new projects. Then early in 2008, I asked Richard to find out if there were other things the IMAGE Project could work on with the women in Kwale village.

After a lengthy conversation, the women implored Richard, "Help us learn how to think." No one had ever asked them thought-provoking, stimulating questions, questions like the ones that my life coach was asking me to answer. We were on a parallel path! The Maasai women felt that they didn't know how to *think* of what was possible in their lives.

When I learned of their request, I thought, *Well, I know from my own experience that life coaching is beneficial. It has helped empower me in my life, and maybe it can benefit them, too.*

But was life coaching over the telephone a real possibility for these women in Tanzania? Would the women be able to get to Iringa, which was a two- to four-hour bus ride from their remote village, for a phone call with someone in America?

Not long after I began wondering about the possibility of making this happen, Scott Nelson, a certified life coach in Minnesota, offered to try making coaching calls with the women. Later that same day, we called Richard to work out the logistics. Life coaching soon became a reality.

In March 2008, we had our first coaching call via cell phone with two women, Mary and Mariam, ages twenty-five and sixty-five, respectively. They were leaders in the village's women's group and were chosen to speak for the other women. They stated their lives in the village were joyful and they felt happy, yet still wanted to keep growing individually. They were hoping to use the conversation from the calls to stretch their thinking and potentially even make small changes in their lives.

At the end of the first call, Mary and Mariam asked, "How can we get to know ourselves?"

The coaching calls with Mary and Mariam continued nearly every other week. Scott, Richard, and I were present on each conference call. Our calls were often interrupted by the loud bellowing of goats and the crying of children in the background. And we'd often get disconnected multiple times in the course of one conversation. Yet we persevered with the coaching sessions. Mary and Mariam loved being asked questions about themselves. Although the women had to learn to trust Scott, they thrived in his sessions due to their deep yearning. Both began opening up and were very capable of relaying what they were learning from these sessions to others in the village.

We were fortunate to learn more about these women's daily lives through the calls. For instance, Mary shared on one call that for her, a typical day began at dawn. She'd first tend the cows and then return to her hut to boil tea. Next, she prepares breakfast for her husband and children. The meal is always *ugali*, which is corn meal mixed with water. After breakfast, she'd go to the farm to work in the fields with a hand hoe. Later, she'd clean vegetables and prepare food for the evening meal. When the cows were herded back to the village in the evening, she'd milk them again.

Around this same time, Richard reported to me that many of the girls we were helping didn't return to school after vacation breaks. If he saw one of the girls during a visit to her village, he'd asked, "Why aren't you in school?"

"My father is not in the village," came the reply, or "My mother does not have any money." Richard realized that the girls' absenteeism was related to the fact that the men of the village made all the decisions. Richard talked to the women, trying to help them realize how important it was to send their children to school. But the women complained that it was too far for the children to walk to school—sometimes three to five miles one way.

The women also told him that families only had the proceeds from the milk from the goats for school money, and there was not enough to help the girls. Finally, they said, the final say on all financial decisions lay with the men. Even if a mother wanted her girl child to go to school but the father didn't, his decision would stand. This was the situation of women and girls in villages like Kwale.

As the coaching calls continued, Mary and Mariam said that other women wanted to learn how to earn more money so they could support their children in school. They would go to work on other farms if they were able, but they wouldn't be able to keep up with their own work if they did.

During the fifth coaching call, the women revealed there was no food or porridge served at the school. Also, children were arriving late each day because they had to walk so far. We brainstormed about how to address some of these problems, and then the women came up with their own idea—perhaps the children could stay at the school overnight. They decided to ask the chief if he would agree to it. First, Mary and Mariam sought advice from Scott as to the best way to go about asking the chief. After discussing this, they decided to go to the chief as a group, an approach that they felt would give each of them more of the courage they needed to speak.

At the next coaching call, we learned that the chief hadn't thought it would be safe to leave the children at the school, so we decided the problem would have to be solved another way. During the call, the women asked, "What if we had our own school?" We quickly learned that they could start clearing the land the following week. Most importantly, the chief had welcomed the new proposal.

The women helped with every part of the process. They were even excited about helping the construction team. They carried water from the river to a large drum to be used for making bricks, for example. When they reported back to us about their progress, they said they were thankful for the coaching calls. "We were in darkness," they said, "but now we are in light."

They were beginning to understand the importance of themselves as individuals. They were learning through the coaching that, within themselves, they had all of the answers to the questions they confronted in their lives. All they had to do was listen and create a space to find them.

CHAPTER 8

Making Progress

You gain strength, courage, and confidence by every experience in which you really stop to look fear in the face. You must do the thing you think you cannot do.

—Eleanor Roosevelt

I headed back to Tanzania at the end of June 2008. The group I was traveling with had hoped to arrive in time to work on the new school in Kwale. But because there was so much excitement and interest in the school, it was built in record time. The men even offered to help clear the land, but the women insisted that they wanted to complete the task. When we arrived one month after the building had begun, the one-room brick school was up and the cement floor had just been poured.

On the first day we visited the village, Richard asked the women to think of a name for their school. They called his cell phone later, saying they couldn't come up with a name. He said, "Try harder and call us back!" That very night, they called with a name—it would be called the Namnyaki Primary School—the school of blessings.

The following day, we again visited Kwale. Our goal was to distribute some used shoes we had brought for the children, as well as to take photos of the children for their sponsors, measure all of them for uniforms, and hand out midwife kits to the women. Many women and children came from neighboring villages, and it was challenging to achieve these goals with so many people around. Our actions must have appeared almost comical as we tried to organize the children into rows. But after many laughs from our group as well as the Maasai women, we succeeded.

Next we drove to the village of Kichangani to determine whether they had projects that they wanted help with. The women of the village sang and danced as we slowly walked to the church. They seemed comfortable with our presence. The small brick church was decorated in typical Maasai fashion; tiny triangular pieces of colorful fabric with frayed edges hung from a string that crisscrossed and draped from the ceiling. On the brick wall was an old blackboard with unfamiliar writing on it.

The chief entered and began singing, swaying from side to side, all the while smiling ear to ear. The women joyfully joined in the singing. Grey-haired and fairly old, the chief had an air of kindness about him. This impression was borne out when he spoke through Richard, our interpreter.

We sat at the front of the church and the women sat on benches scattered throughout the space. We began by asking the women to tell us about their daily lives. They seemed eager to speak, even though this was the first time we had met with them. They started by saying, "As you know, we are women from the Maasai, and one of the things we do is make jewelry. But we need customers. And some of the elder women's greatest desire is to read and write."

Other women said:

"We keep chickens and do some gardening."

"We irrigate by carrying water in the buckets."

"We have adult education, and we have a blackboard to read from and write on."

One woman explained that she rose at four in the morning and walked several miles to milk the cows. When she returned with the milk, she'd take a pail to fetch water for the small calves and goats that were kept at home. She sometimes had to travel a long distance five times a day to get enough water. Additionally, she filled vessels with milk for her children, fetched firewood, and gathered vegetables. Her days were long and filled with many tasks.

"I have one burning issue in the village," she said, "especially in December and January. The government bans us from going to carry water from the river, because of crocodiles that sometimes kill people. We have to go further away from the main river to get water."

Another woman said, "The number of herds of goats is decreasing, because they are dying from lack of good nourishment and disease due to the recent drought in this area. Food is a problem. It's a challenge, and we wish to focus more on agriculture, but we are very new to it."

The chief said, "I participated in one of the coaching sessions with the women of Kwale. I would also like if that project could come to this village. I would like to do the same thing that is happening in Kwale with the goat and chicken projects. Our environment is very difficult for us. We would like to improve the lifestyle of our village. The men know that your goal is to help the women, and we are also ready to support the women. Whatever you decide, we are ready to do our part."

After these amazing reports from the women and the

chief, Zach Schultz, an American in our group could not help but ask, "What do the men do?"

"It's not easy to understand," a woman answered. "Some ten years ago, the men were responsible for keeping the houses in good shape. But these days, although some men are becoming supportive, other men leave almost everything for the women to do."

At the end of our conversation, which lasted an hour, the women stated they believed that knowing how to read and write would help them learn how to focus, set goals, and have direction in their lives. We left the village feeling we had established the beginning of a working relationship. We had many ideas of projects that they and we could start.

The following day, we drove for two hours over a dusty, bumpy road to visit the Image Secondary School (a separate entity from the IMAGE Project). Nearly fifty young Maasai girls were waiting outside the school. They greeted us warmly with dancing and singing. We divided them into small groups to hear more about their backgrounds and families, needs and challenges.

Most girls came from very large families. One stated that her father had forty-two children. There were so many, she said, that he didn't even know their names.

Another girl requested a blanket. She was suffering from tuberculosis, and she typically felt cold at night. We took detailed notes so we could send this information on to the sponsors who would later generously support these girls.

CHAPTER 9

Changing Lives

If you change the way you look at things,
the things you look at change.

    —Wayne W. Dyer

In November 2008, I traveled again to Tanzania. Our group
of six was going to evaluate the secondary scholarship project, along with the chicken and goat projects, and to visit the
Maasai villages. I was grateful to have Linda Cullen from Fifty
Lanterns International traveling with us. She would distribute solar lanterns to the women in the villages so they could
have light for the difficult labor they had to complete in the
darkness of night and early morning.

As we traveled in a bus to Kwale for church service on
Sunday, Richard asked one of our group, Mike Foley, if he
would be willing to give the sermon—in an hour! Mike swal-
lowed hard and replied, "Absolutely!" Mike quickly grabbed
some paper and pen and began scribbling notes for what
would shortly become a magnificent sermon.

When we arrived at the church, women who were becoming increasingly familiar to me surrounded us. There were
only a few men present. As was their custom, the women
greeted us with much singing and dancing upon our arrival.

As we entered the church, my eyes drifted to the uneven hole in the handmade brick wall that served as a window. We each took our spot on the uneven earth floor beneath us, seated on handmade stools made of a dark wood.

The stools were pushed close together in the small space where about seventy-five people were gathered. I looked up at the simple makeshift altar at the front, which was bare but for a small piece of fabric draped over it. The day was very hot and the room was stifling. Although no air moved through that church, I could feel the Holy Spirit moving through all of us that day. We knew God was in our midst.

In the afternoon, we first visited the Namnyaki Primary School. We brought several duffle bags of school supplies, including maps to hang on the walls and schoolbooks donated by our generous sponsors. At one point, I looked toward the back of the schoolroom to see Chief Salehe pointing to countries on the map and asking for clarification from Deb Schultz, a retired school teacher who had coordinated our school supply efforts. The map of the world intrigued the chief. Many small children milled about the room, behaving just as you'd expect American children would in an exciting gathering of adults. They were learning to say "thank you" to us in English, taught to them by Efiki, one of our star secondary students. Their beaming smiles communicated their pride in the school. We were warmly welcomed once again.

Around dusk that evening, we experienced the most amazing sight. We were at Mary's hut, testing her solar light, making sure it worked. The herds of branded cattle belonging to the Maasai were arriving. They bellowed and stirred up billows of dust as they made their way into the village from all directions. This happened every night at the same time.

Small herds of goats joined the migration into the center of the tiny village, adding to the huge commotion.

Amid the noise, people were running to herd the cattle into corrals; it was like a scene from an old *Bonanza* movie. The calves stayed behind in the village each day while their mothers grazed in the surrounding bush. When their mothers reappeared, the calves struggled to rejoin them, but the women attempted to keep them from nursing until the cows were milked. Simultaneously, other women appeared, each carrying fifteen- to eighteen-inch-long orange gourds decorated with cowhides and colorful beads, which they used to milk the cows. The scene had started with a huge commotion and now was ending peacefully with each baby calf finding its mother.

After the cattle had been settled into their corrals, the women wanted to show us their homes, which they had constructed themselves from cow dung and dirt. These one-room structures ranged in size from five-by-five to ten-by-ten feet. Most homes had little in them; their main purpose was to provide a roof over the family members' heads while they slept. We learned later that the mothers and the children slept in a single bed, and sometimes the father, too.

One woman had nailed worn-out shoes to each side of the doorway so she could hang a covering over the doorway for privacy. Most of the homes had bare earthen floors. Some had chickens roosting in the corners, and others had day-old baby goats tied to the handmade wooden beds for protection during the day while the mother goats were in the bush.

In the morning, we returned to Kwale to meet with the women to learn more about their lives. We sat under a large acacia tree in the red dirt. Some Tanzanians say that the acacia tree holds up the sky because it appears that the tree grows upside down, with the roots holding up the sky. The goats wandered around us, braying, while children cried. Even with the distractions, I could hear the pain and see the courage of the women as they spoke. They took turns telling their stories. None of us were prepared to hear the depth of oppression these women experienced in every aspect of their lives.

Mariam, the oldest wife to the chief, started by saying, "As Maasai women, we have no say about anything in our lives. We are unable to inherit property and have no say in our children's future. If our children go to secondary school and need something, we have to ask our husbands for help. He may say no. He may say, 'Do this. Do that.' If we don't, we may be beaten. He may say, 'You women have enough money.'"

Judith, a sister to the chief, then began to tell her story. Her mother had died when she was young. All of the property belonging to her parents was taken over by her relatives, as is the custom. They raised her, but she had a difficult life. She received no education and had no rights or property.

She said, "I can't explain it. I have never seen love from any person. God is the only one who loves me."

Judith said her grown daughter died in childbirth, and she was responsible for raising her daughter's children. She wanted to know if we could help her educate her orphaned grandchildren. She was trying to support her grandsons in secondary school by milking cows and gardening. One boy was staying at home because he was having much difficulty at school. We agreed to consider how we could help her in the future.

Monika waved her arms, talking in Swahili. She wanted to say something. "As of this moment, I have a cow especially for my baby, Deborah. The money earned from the milk of the cow will be saved for Deborah's education. The only thing that my baby daughter can inherit from me is education." So Monika will save the money she gets from milking the cow for Deborah. She hides the money in a hole she digs in the red dirt so no one can find it.

Mary stated, "When I was forced to get married, I had been thinking of education. But nobody was willing to send me to school. If I had an education, I would know what to do with my children. I am trying to work on a small business project to make sure I get more money to take care of my sick child. But when the men came back from another village, they took over my business. When the plants were ready for marketing, some men came and took the property, leaving me with nothing."

Although the chief in Kwale was not Mary's biological father, he gave her a place to stay with her children when she ran away from the home she previously shared with her husband. This chief's humanity towards women makes him very different from most Maasai chiefs in other villages.

Two hours into our discussion under the acacia tree, Maria waved a photograph in the air. "Look at that fat goat. Do you see it?" she asked. "I decided, after experiencing oppression, that no one is going to help me. I was raising chickens. Then I decided to sell the chickens and buy this goat."

Tasiana quietly interjected to our group, "You can see she was beaten. Can you see the long scar on her arm?"

We nodded our heads yes. The conversation was getting very tough to hear, but our group was open to listening.

Maria went on, "I bought the goat and took care of it. When my project earned enough money, I bought five more goats. But some men came and took all the goats. I tried to say, 'Don't take them, because these are my goats. Don't sell them. I want to improve the house. I have seven children with one room.' But they didn't listen.

"I was supposed to stay outside at night and sleep in the dirt, so the children could sleep inside," Maria continued. "When I was trying to say, 'These goats are mine,' I was beaten. There was no money for me. I want to cry now as I tell you this story. It is very painful. I am still trying to build my new house. This is the fifth year of my effort to improve my home."

Maria continues to sleep outside at night in the red dirt.

As we left the protection of the tree branches that afternoon, the women hugged us, saying they felt free and better after having had someone listen to them. They said that no one had ever listened to or cared about their stories before. It was a new blessing for each of them to find their own voice. We had realized that the most important part we could play for many of these women was to listen.

Even though we had said very little that afternoon, our facial expressions in response to their stories and our tears at certain junctures in their stories gave validation to women who had never been validated in their lives. We didn't offer solutions. We just listened. I felt that we needed to let the powerful stories rest in our hearts for awhile before trying to help them solve their problems.

Later that day I heard through Richard that a Maasai mother was at the Lutheran Center, wanting to meet with us about her daughter. As we sat outside, the mother told this story:

"My sister's child is age twelve, the same age as this daughter who is here with me. She was married to an older man, and after some time she bore a child who had problems. After two months, the baby was taken away from her, and my niece was told to go and take care of the cattle. She never saw the baby again. Then my niece had another baby who had physical problems, and again they took that baby from her. I watched how hard it is for her to endure this. I want my own daughter to have a different life.

"I came to know of your program, but I couldn't get my older daughter in, because her father forced her to get married. My daughter argued and said, 'No, I don't want to get married.' But already the men were there to marry her. I went to my husband and pleaded, 'I will do whatever it takes to save this daughter and get her to school.'

"Although I am aged," she continued, "I want my children to go to primary school, and I want my daughters to be educated. Once the men know that someone will stand up to them, they release the girls to go to school. I believe that education is the only possible solution to the problem of early marriages.

Although I am here today, even my husband doesn't know. He will not react positively. Even the man who came with a cow for my daughter knows I don't want him to marry my child, because she has to go to school. Even if my husband says that he will abandon the children, I say, 'Yes, it is better for you to abandon them, because then they get an education.'"

When she looks at the life of Maasai women, she feels they are really in bondage compared to the women of other tribes. She felt very strongly that she needed to give her daughters choices in their lives so they could shape their own futures, and the only path to having choices was education.

As I listened to her story, my heart broke. I wept for so many women that day—women who showed so much conviction in their views, so much courage to reveal these challenges, and so much hope for their daughters.

As I recorded my impressions in my journal that evening, I felt the Holy Spirit in my heart and understood even more clearly God's calling for my life. I was there to listen with my heart and then carry the stories of those who have no voice to others who can make a difference in their lives.

A few days later, we visited the Image Secondary School, which was about two hours from Iringa. The Maasai girls who were in the secondary classes greeted us with traditional singing and dancing. They were very excited to see us and expressed gratitude for being able to pursue an education. There were then nearly fifty Maasai girls at the school of about six hundred other Tanzanian students.

We divided the girls into small groups in order to learn more about the issues they were facing. Many were orphans, having lost one or both parents. Many had arrived at the school without any personal items, and most needed books and other supplies. Despite these setbacks, the girls were flourishing and they were participating in their education.

Having completed our evaluations of the secondary school project and the chicken and goat projects, our group left Tanzania with new knowledge and with heavy hearts. After our departure, Tasiana and Richard continued visiting the villages, spending time with the girls at school and working on the projects in the villages.

CHAPTER 10

Building Relationships

The glory of friendship is not the outstretched hand, nor the kindly smile, nor the joy of companionship; it's the spiritual inspiration that comes to one when she discovers that someone else believes in her and is willing to trust her as her friend.

—Ralph Waldo Emerson

I had been struggling with how much time I was investing in this portion of my life; I wanted a better balance, and also felt the need for streamlining our projects in Africa so that we created the most impact with the least amount of funds. We needed to have a clear and simple focus for the projects we adopted. I was hopeful my next trip would clarify our focus.

A group of five left for Tanzania in November 2009; it consisted of me and four others, some of whom had traveled with me previously. Our goals sounded simple: to listen to villagers in the areas where we were working in order to find out what they needed, to visit a new village, and to evaluate all of our projects.

The women and girls greeted us warmly when we arrived in Kwale. They were excited to speak the English words they had learned the previous year. Even Chief Salehe joined us for the worship service at the Namnyaki School.

The children huddled around and found their places on the dusty floor. During our presentation, we asked questions and learned that four of the women—Maria, Judith, Esther, and Mary—attend classes every day after completing their afternoon chores. They were so proud of their accomplishments. Our efforts were reaching farther than we had hoped or anticipated.

We divided the women into groups at the school that hot day in November and listened as they told us the status of their agricultural and animal projects.

It was a surprise to hear one woman who said, "We can't do both goats and chickens—just one or the other—it's too much work." The remark made me aware of how I needed to apply that approach to my own life: not doing too much at once. I continued to learn every time I listened to the women.

Some of the women voiced the challenges they were facing with the chicken projects. One stated, "Something long and skinny is taking the baby chicks." Later we would learn that it was probably a mongoose. "Large hawks swoop down only inches from us and steal the baby chicks," another said. We consulted with the women to find solutions to these problems.

As we sat under the stark acacia tree, the only thing that offered escape from the hot sun, the chief visited with us and acknowledged that many of the girls who had been married too young were having serious problems. "I'm happy that with these changes the women are now being taken more seriously by the men, and many are being asked questions by the men for the first time in their lives," he said. This showed important progress for our programs.

Gwen Thomas and I interviewed Mariam, the oldest wife to the chief. As always, this was accomplished through an interpreter. Mariam expressed her realization that the Maasai culture was changing. The one aspect she wanted to retain, she said, was their traditional clothing, of which she was very proud. The women wear brightly colored clothing with a lot of decorative beaded jewelry. They also expand their earlobes as a sign of beauty. We assured her that no one wanted them to lose this aspect of their culture.

Mariam went on to say that she had given birth to seven children, one of whom had died. Her dream for her only living daughters, Jeska and Joyce, was that one day they would have the skills to find employment, so they would be spared the hardship she has suffered living a traditional life as a Maasai woman.

"If a girl has education, she can lead the family better and lead her own life," she said. She told us, in essence, that education gives girls the power to stand strong and argue for their rights, to receive respect. We heard reflected in Mariam's thoughts the idea that if one educates a girl, the village is changed.

Later we visited Image Secondary School, where the girls were just finishing their exams. We broke into groups, so we could give more of the girls a chance to share. We wanted to find out what was working for them and where they needed help. As we were checking their names off the list, we noticed two girls who were not on the list, but who were obviously attending school. Richard indicated we would talk with them separately. They looked nervous.

Many of the girls said they were orphans and had no one to help them, but now it was becoming obvious that many were being sent by their uncles or brothers. This demonstrated to us that even the men of the villages were aware of the benefits of educating the Maasai girls and desired that opportunity for more girls. This, however, wasn't the case for all girls.

One of the girls didn't want to share in the group discussion; she wanted to talk privately. She said she couldn't go home at break because her father had told her that he would not feed her. According to the girl, he said, "If education is so important, use it as food." Then he chased her away, telling her she wasn't worth anything to him.

Next we spoke with the two mysterious students who were not on our list. We asked them how they came to be at the school. Evidently, a boy had told them to go directly to the school, and that he would talk to the headmaster on their behalf. Both girls, one twelve and the other fourteen years old, had been set up for pre-arranged marriages, and they wept as they told their stories of wanting a better life for themselves.

The courage these girls showed in striking out on their own, seeking a better life, was rewarded. Donations to the IMAGE Project covered their enrollment, and they currently are students at the school.

After spending a few days in Iringa, we returned to Kwale with Dr. Andy Hart, a local veterinarian, who gave a seminar on caring for chickens, both in the village and nearby Kichangani. He taught them how to vaccinate their chickens against Newcastle and Kideri disease, which takes 60 percent of their flocks each year. The women in Kwale had not been aware that we were coming, so there was a lot of commotion when we arrived. Some of the women were in the fields, some were tending the children, and others were in their homes. They gathered as we found our places under the same large acacia tree, along with the sheep and goats.

Dr. Hart requested a baby chick be brought to him so he could demonstrate how to dip the chick in gentian violet dye to prevent the large birds from stealing it. Animals know that anything brightly colored is dangerous or poisonous, and they avoid it. Eventually the baby chick would mature and grow new feathers, Dr. Hart assured the women, returning to its natural color. In the meantime, it would live and someday provide nourishment for a family that has so little.

That same day, the women told the group about the crocodile problem at the river. A few days earlier, the boys had taken the cows down to the river to drink and encountered a crocodile basking in the sun. They threw rocks at it until it swam away, but they were sure it would be back. The rains would come soon, giving the crocodiles deep water in which to hide, but for now they could be seen in the shallow river water. They hoped to construct a fence as protection. They knew the danger was very real, because a crocodile had killed Judith's brother as he walked along the river one day.

In the evening, Tasiana, Richard, and I spent time discussing the projects and reasoning through solutions to the problems that the village women had identified. Tasiana had started personal-growth groups in the villages. According to her, as a result of these meetings, the girls were beginning to take a stand for their futures. They were feeling more comfortable arguing with the chief, for example, about why they wanted to go to school.

Still, the women and girls struggled with problems. They lacked study skills, for example, and more seriously, many had emotional issues. Many of the girls suffered from a lack of self-esteem. They believed they were inferior, because that is what they had been taught and what had been reinforced by their culture. Others had difficulty concentrating because of circumstances at home. Several had had to leave their duties as caretakers for their grandmothers to come to school, and now these girls felt responsible, because no one was gathering food or meeting their families' other needs.

Many girls were also overwhelmed with feelings of loss and abandonment by their parents. Their grandmothers had been the only ones who had shown them love, and now they were apart from that support while they attended school. Others were traumatized by the experiences they faced in order to arrive at the school. For each of them, opportunities had arisen for them to have better lives, but they were still left to choose between tradition and education. Choosing education often left others in their families—particularly the grandmothers—in difficult circumstances.

Under Tasiana's guidance, the girls had learned to role-play, which proved very helpful for them as they began to express their needs. Some of the roles they took on were that of the disapproving father, or that of the oppressed young girl. In the beginning, the girls had a hard time using words to describe their experiences, but role-playing provided a new and easier outlet for their buried emotions.

CHAPTER 11

Coming Around the Bend

Similarities create friendships,
while differences hold them together.

—Anonymous

During this trip, I was eager to visit the Maasai village of Mhuva, which was new to our project and was where Mary and Monika had moved. Drought conditions in Kwale had pushed many villagers to live in new places. The day before we were to travel to the new village, we experienced the opposite of the drought: flash-flooding. We knew that the rains could be very dangerous if we should be caught in them while in the mountains.

Because of our great wish to visit with our friends, we decided to undertake the journey, so we left at six in the morning and arrived in Morogoro around noon. We grabbed some water, fruit, and bread, and expected to go on driving about ninety minutes into the bush. We figured we would arrive in the village around 1:30 that afternoon, have a short visit, and still get back to Morogoro by dusk. We were wrong.

As the vehicle started climbing into the hills, the road became narrower and the dust became heavy. As it neared one thirty, Richard called Mary to see if the road was still passable.

"You are very close," she said.

We pressed on, and the road became even narrower. Even though it was summer in Tanzania, the trees were changing to autumnal colors, with leaves covering the forest ground, just as in Minnesota. Then the terrain changed again—this time to tropical foliage, and soon thereafter to granite-like rock formations. We kept climbing the narrow mountain road in our old Toyota vehicle, realizing more and more the relativity of Mary's use of the word "close." We called Mary again.

"Don't despair—you are very close," she reassured us again. "I am sitting alongside the road, so you will know where to turn."

Don't despair, we're almost there became our mantra.

At each corner I eagerly looked for Mary. My watch showed 2:30, then 3:30. Still no Mary. Richard called her again.

"You are very close; do not despair," she repeated. In my heart, I felt anxious.

We drove through a small village that had obviously been struck by severe poverty. From our view on the road, we saw, down to the right and in a valley, only tin roofs. I thought, *How does anyone live with so little?* I still had an uneasy feeling—and still no sign of Mary.

Finally, just as we came down from the mountain path, a most beautiful sight appeared. Experiencing the view was reminiscent of looking out over a green, lush valley as one comes down from a mountain pass in Colorado. And there, sitting alongside the road, was Mary, patiently waiting for us, smiling ear to ear. A man was there with her, and the two of them boarded our vehicle with the bags of vegetables Mary had bought in the village. There was much laughter and many smiles, but we still had to get to the village. We drove another

Tasiana Njau and Richard Lubawa

Richard Lubawa visiting a Maasai village

A Maasai family in Tanzania

Maasai girls and women seated on a dried cow hide, preparing to feed the baby from a gourd decorated with beads

Tasiana teaching an older woman to write her name for the first time

Mary, the mother of Malaky

Women from the village of Kwale at the Namnyaki School

The Namnyaki School children in their new uniforms

Maasai women and children attending a church service

A gathering of women at Kwale Lutheran Church

Young students with their new story books

Maasai women attending reading and writing classes at Namnyaki School

Monika milking a cow to feed her daughter

A home in a Maasai village

A herd of cows owned by the Maasai

Maria standing among the young calves

New students being read to by Efiki, a recent graduate (photo courtesy of Linda Cullen)

Students at Image Secondary School

A flock of chickens, arriving from a nearby village to be raised by the women

A chicken coop built by the Maasai women

Secondary students with their new backpacks filled with school supplies

The families who moved to Mhuva

The women of Kwale village

Chief Salehe admiring his new solar light

Chief Salehe sitting at a new school desk

An amazing field of onions and corn

Sarah, one of our students with her son, Endrew (photo courtesy of Gwen Thomas)

A beautiful Maasai woman (photo courtesy of Gwen Thomas)

Learning to read and write at Namnyaki School

A happy young student

Maasai women herding goats with their new school books (photo courtesy of Terry Jensen)

"I feel empowered just holding a pencil." (photo courtesy of Tasiana Njau)

Judith with a goat that belongs to the women's project

Mary, Debra, and Malaky

Tasiana's graduation from college, October 2010

New students

Emanueli Mselemu and Chiefs Salehe, Alolo and Lembile attending a meeting in Kwale

"I've heard of this thing called education. Do you think it will help my granddaughter?"

Fields of onions, corn, and beans in Kwale village; these fields are part of the agricultural project started by the women

Proud women among their crop of corn

Excited secondary students displaying their new school books

Paulina, one of the first Maasai girls to graduate from our program; she is employed as an assistant physical therapist

Maasai men attending the meeting at Kwale in support of educating their daughters, sisters, and nieces

Primary students dressed with new uniforms

Heading down the cow path toward the waterfall in Pommern

twenty minutes down a dusty road, until it became impass-
able for our vehicle.

There was no way our vehicle could drive into the village
in the bush, so we parked along the road and started walking.
We moved through the bush, and found the walk as lovely as
a fall walk through a forest in Minnesota. As we turned the
corner into the village, singing and smiling faces met us. We
had finally arrived in Mhuva after nearly five hours of traveling. We were safe. Our appearance seemed to validate our
relationship with the women who were counting on our
presence. They were so proud and happy we were there. All
of the men had gathered to celebrate with us as well. We felt
instantly welcomed.

Richard asked each woman to stand with her children, so
Linda from Fifty Lanterns could hand out a solar lantern to
each one. She also gave one to the chief, who seemed happy to
receive the gift. The men were given lanterns as well, which
they could use while herding their cows at dusk or dawn.

Just as we were feeling at ease, Richard said the chief
wanted to talk to me. Taken off guard, I cautiously approached
him.

The chief asked, "Could you take two of my daughters to
the secondary school to give them a chance at education?" I
happily agreed to fulfill his request, realizing my fears had
been for nothing.

Our short visit reconfirmed our commitment to work
with the women. It came to an end far too soon, but we had to
get back on the long road to Morogoro, and it was getting late
in the day. Everyone followed us back to the edge of the forest,
to the spot where our vehicle was parked. We were very sad
to leave the lovely place we had just entered, and even then I

was filled with gratitude for having met the villagers. We had witnessed what happens when families are able to move from lives of hardship to places where there is hope, and the difficulties of leaving their loved ones behind to begin new lives.

The trip had its intended results. We were able to explore some of their challenges and we understood in what direction the IMAGE Project was moving. I looked forward to putting into practice the life lessons I'd learned from the Maasai women. As had my previous trips, this trip changed my life, working alongside courageous, bold, and inspiring Maasai women.

CHAPTER 12

A Full Circle

God, you have called your servants into ventures of which we
cannot see the ending, by paths as yet untrodden through perils
unknown. Give us faith to go out with good courage; not knowing
where we go but only that your hand is leading us and your love
supporting us. Amen.

—A prayer

During my trip the year before, I realized that our relationship with the Maasai living around Iringa was the backbone
of this project. I had made the decision on my way home in
2009 to deepen my relationship with the Maasai women
and girls. I made that happen by calling Tasiana soon after
I got home. After getting a progress report on the girls from
her, I asked for Mary's cell phone number in Mhuva, the tiny
remote village in the mountains we had visited and where
she and her family were living at the time.

Tasiana sent me some Swahili phrases to use, and
between Rosetta Stone and my Swahili book, I took a chance
and called Mary shortly after New Year's. It was a short call
during which we laughed at each other—I was trying to learn
Swahili and she was trying to learn English, so a lot of it was
just joyful laughter. She was so surprised by my call that,

when we hung up, she immediately called Tasiana to convey her amazement that I had contacted her.

Mary also reported to Tasiana that she and seven other women now have twelve chickens and three goats. They had applied their training from Dr. Hart whom we had arranged to visit Kwale earlier in the year, and they had vaccinated their chickens and goats. Her children were attending primary school and she was continuing to practice reading and writing. Mary was, and is, extremely motivated, striving to improve her economic status and provide an education for her children.

We continued these calls throughout the year. Whenever I could get through to Mary—usually on Sundays—we talked a little. Basically, I was saying the same things. "How are the children? How are the chickens? Are you studying English?" I enjoyed it and felt we really connected, even though we didn't always have a lot to say to one another. Because of my regular telephone contacts with Mary, the women of Kwale came to realize that we were involved in an ongoing, mutual effort between them and the supporters of the IMAGE Project.

Throughout 2009, Tasiana continued to work in the villages with the young girls. With her counseling background, she began to set up group growth meetings with the girls to encourage them. She also modeled how they could provide emotional support to one another. Some of the girls had difficulty learning to trust others, while others found their environment to be a safe place to express themselves.

When Tasiana visited the Namnyaki Primary School at Kwale, she found the children doing very well with their studies. Even though it was a five-and-a-half-mile walk to the government school each way, they returned to the Namnyaki

Primary School in the afternoon for extra classes. And they were full of energy. When she asked them from where their energy came, one of the students said, "We envy our sisters who joined secondary school. We are studying hard in order to do well in our exams so we can someday attend secondary school."

Prior to my departure for Tanzania in the fall of 2010, Tasiana called me one day, saying that Mary had returned to Kwale from Mhuva. Tasiana found her near her home, holding what appeared to be a tiny three-month-old baby. Tasiana was shocked. Mary hadn't said anything to anyone about a baby. It was a little boy, and she told Tasiana that she was waiting for me to arrive to name him.

When I found out, I thought, *What a privilege! But what would I name him?* I decided to look in the Bible, and the first name that jumped out at me was Malachi. I was so sure that it was the perfect name that I didn't look any further. Later, when we arrived in Iringa and told Tasiana the name, she quickly told me that Malachi translated to Swahili means "Milkie." It was not a good name for a future chief! In the end, the name morphed into Malaky, with an accent on the middle syllable. Mary was pleased, and Malaky, with his large eyes, broadly smiled his approval.

In mid-October 2010, I arrived in Iringa with a group of three other Americans after the long journey from Dar es Salaam on treacherous roads filled with construction crews. We found the views along the way dramatic: low mountains, rock formations, and valleys filled with baobab trees. The area was dry from drought. Our route took us through a national park and we saw giraffes, elephants, and zebras not too far into the bush alongside the road.

I welcomed the feel of the hot dry air, and felt glad to see the familiar red dirt and the colorful clothing of the Tanzanian people who thronged near the roads. Anytime we exited the vehicle, welcoming smiles and "Jambo! Karibu!" (Hello! Welcome!) greeted us.

The Saturday after we arrived, we were excited to be invited to attend Tasiana's graduation from Tumaini University, where we met her family. Also present were Anna, a Maasai mother, and many other of Tasiana's friends, both Maasai and relatives. Nearly eight hundred and fifty students graduated that day, and although it was difficult to catch a glimpse of Tasiana, she texted me during the ceremony to say she was so happy we were there. She expressed herself beautifully: "Now you can see the fruits of your harvest in helping me reach my dream of graduating."

Shortly after she received her diploma, we learned that Mary (and her then still-unnamed son) had arrived at the university from Kwale, having been urged to attend the graduation by her husband, Mateyo. It was quite a special occasion to have Mary present to see Tasiana reach her dream. The celebration carried over into the evening, with dinner at Tasiana's home with all of our Maasai friends, including current students who were so proud of Tasiana's achievement. I could only imagine they were hopeful that they, too, would someday graduate from college.

Early on Monday, we packed up our vehicle to drive to Kwale, where we would attend a meeting in the village with the women. We had heard that some men might come, too. But first, we had to stop in the market for several boxes of bottled water. Richard had mentioned earlier that someone had called him and was requesting to meet us. He told them to be in the market when we arrived.

After getting out of our vehicle, we turned the corner, and there stood an older Maasai girl and two smaller girls. They were dressed in traditional Maasai clothing, so we recognized them at once. The older girl requested a scholarship for the younger girls, as their parents were trying to arrange their marriages. We moved our group into a nearby alley for privacy, where we took their photos and got a few more details. We asked them to call Richard in a few days, which they agreed to do.

Then we started out for Kwale, a trip that would take about an hour and a half of driving over the mountain range, through the valley, and through more construction. We finally arrived in the little village of Kwale. Mary and her baby were with us in our vehicle, along with two other young Maasai women who had managed to get to Iringa to see Tasiana graduate. We took the opportunity to talk to Mary about her life.

Mary, who was twenty-eight at the time, said, "My dream is for my children to be educated so someday they will help me in life. Girls were always supposed to be married, but now they have opportunities for education. Years ago, when you started helping the girls, the men thought the girls would receive an education and then leave their culture—and their families and villages. That, however, has not happened.

"What they see are girls like Upendo, one of the IMAGE Project's first students, now attending Tumaini University. When Upendo goes home to visit, she shaves her head as the other women do, and goes out to tend to the goats. Now the men and women see that their culture is really not threatened and the girls will come back to their heritage."

The girls expressed to us their desire to help others in their village.

Mary continued, saying, "My husband, Mateyo, is very supportive of education and encourages me to learn more and to help our children."

We knew that Mateyo's support would make a big difference for the future of Mary's children: Mateyo was the son of the chief, and would become chief himself one day. Mary told us of her dreams of improving her home and having one room for her and Mateyo, one room for the children, and a sitting room. They were currently sharing a two-room hut.

There had been a mix-up in communication, and although we went to the school for our planned meeting, everyone else was at the church. We found our spots in the school as the children started to congregate. I was amazed to see several men enter the school one by one and find their places at the back of the room. In short order, the school filled up, and to my astonishment the crowd included nearly fifteen to twenty men.

There must have been seventy women in attendance, most with little babies tied in shawls on their backs. There also were at least fifty children present, some clinging to the bars of the windows from outside, hoping to catch a few words of what would be a very important discussion about their future. Throughout the meeting, the babies were tended to easily by the women. Then the chief entered, and behind him came his five wives and his three new wives; one who was only fourteen years old with a small child.

The classroom was small, only about twenty by thirty-five feet, and so the space was tightly packed. Richard started the meeting with a prayer in the Maasai language. Then he asked each person to stand and tell us where she or he was from and if she or he had a daughter or relative in the program. I wrote down names, and I couldn't believe what I was hearing. There were men from as far away as Dar es Salaam (ten hours or more by bus), as well as fathers, uncles, mothers, and aunts to the girls in our program. The largest Maasai man I have ever seen stood up and introduced himself. He was seated next to two other chiefs. I could see the bush knife at the large man's side, and he seemed agitated and angry about something. But I couldn't understand him, as he spoke in Maasai. He seemed to have much to say and started to speak, but was interrupted by Richard, who said he should wait to speak until the meeting started. I found the large man intriguing, and I couldn't help but wonder if the men were actually in support of girls' education or if they held differing opinions. We would soon find out.

As the meeting progressed, the large Maasai spoke again. This time he loudly and firmly said that he had heard that his sisters "were studying hard" and that he was glad. A Maasai university student, Immanuel, interpreted for us: "We Maasai have been given a gift of education. We need to start educating our daughters. We all have to work with the Americans to educate our girls." His statement surprised me, but it was wonderful to hear.

Later I would find out that he was one of the brothers who had loaned the bus fare to the four little girls we had met the previous year in order for them to travel to Iringa. Upon their arrival in Iringa, the girls had said they were fighting for their rights and liberation. Now I knew who stood behind them, and I could see that no man was going to argue or stop this man from educating girls from his village.

The meeting lasted nearly four hours, but it seemed shorter. I tried to explain that even though we had different values and cultures, we each represented a circle. Where our individual circles overlapped was what we had in common. One commonality was a desire to educate girls.

The women who spoke were extremely dignified and spoke eloquently in front of the men—something they rarely were able to do. Every commentary began with a heartfelt expression of thanks to us and to God, who had brought us together. Mariam spoke first, stating that the women were thinking of investing in a milling machine so they could earn extra money to help their daughters.

Anna said she was grateful that we are helping her daughter. She was thinking of ways to pay us back. She had been working on small businesses just to make sure she could contribute to the bus fare for her daughter to return home to visit during school breaks. She thought she could start a chicken project or a small shop to help raise some income.

Another mother stood tall and said, "If we are empowered, I know we can manage to help our daughters."

Then Chief Salehe said in regard to the primary school, "We already have the school, books, and the resources for education. We need to assess what the problem is. Is it the teachers? The mothers? The fathers?"

We were a bit unclear about what he considered to be the problem, but assumed it involved the challenges that the very young children faced in attending school.

There was much talking, interpreting, and positive feedback. The large man said he had heard that his sisters were studying hard and were "not fooling around." Appreciative laughter met this remark.

At one point, Richard mentioned the idea of building a school for Maasai girls. All of the men raised their right arms, as did the women, and they shouted in loud voices, "Hey! Hey!"—their way of agreeing. They said they were willing to give financial support to build a school.

I found the most interesting part of the meeting to be the presence of so many men. They had come to the meeting because they cared about girls, and they wanted change. Up until then, we had rarely heard or seen the men. Other years, they had been present only at a distance at our meetings. We knew that this meeting would be one of the most momentous events of our trip: we had witnessed history being made. The futures of the girls were taking a different course, with the engagement of an extended Maasai community.

The meeting ended with a prayer. We all thanked God for bringing us together and for the path that he would now lead us down—together.

I thought the meeting was over. It appeared to be. But suddenly the large Maasai man came back in the room with six darling little girls. Evidently, unbeknownst to me, they had been part of the group of children hanging around outside the window while we had our meeting. They were six more of his sisters and he wanted us to enroll them in school. Then another man entered with four girls whom he also wanted us to enroll in school. Then a chief approached and said he had a daughter to enroll, but she wasn't present that day. He wondered if we could help her. He seemed very genuine, as did the other men—caring for their daughters and changing the path of their lives.

Later in the day, we went further into the area where the women lived with their families for a lunch under the spreading branches of an acacia tree. We had huge platefuls of pure white rice, some cooked greens with other vegetables for seasoning, a meat sauce with small pieces of chicken and pork, and soda pop or bottled water. We Americans sat together with the village men as guests of honor. The women waited nearby for us to finish eating before they and their children ate.

As I was taking some photos, the large Maasai chief turned back to me with his cell phone in hand and took my photo. Touché! Cell phones are everywhere in Tanzania and so is cell phone photography.

As we finished lunch, an older woman approached Tasiana and me. She was the grandmother of Mary, her grandchild and only living relative. She had raised Mary after her father died and the child's mother had married someone else. Mary has never seen her mother since that time. The previous year, this same grandmother had brought Mary to us, saying, "I have heard of this thing called education. Do you think it will help my granddaughter?"

Mary was doing well in school, the grandmother now told us, but she often cried for her grandmother, and the woman was worried about her. Mary was aware that no one was caring for her grandmother, and the grandmother told us that she was lonely without Mary. She no longer had any energy to work in the fields and felt too old to fight off the hawks that tried to attack the chickens. She didn't even know how old she was. She said the only thing she could do was make beaded crosses, but she couldn't even afford the beads.

At the end of this unhappy conversation, we did not have a solution. However, I bought the two crosses she had with her and ordered some more to help her, if even in a very small way.

Then two Maasai women approached us. One of them

sat down and I noticed that she had a bandage on her leg. She told us a snake with a big head had bitten her the previous year. She wanted me to take a photo of her leg, so she unwrapped the bandage. It was a horrific site, with a lot of infection. We agreed that the snake that had attacked her must have been a cobra. Evidently, unlike Western medicine, the traditional healing practices of Maasai had some special medicine for these types of snakebites; had she not received it, she would have died from the bite. The next day, I provided her with some cleansing pads and antiseptic cream. Without any medical connections, there was nothing else we could do.

Just then, the women approached me as a group and said they wanted to honor a friend of mine, Katherine Slaikeu Nolan, who at age thirty-two had died in May 2010 after a long battle with cancer. Previously, we had told them that Katherine had requested that donations be made toward their projects in her memory. They had been speechless at the time. They couldn't get over how someone who didn't even know them would help them after she died. This was their way of honoring her spirit.

They had made four thick, beaded crosses, six to seven inches tall, with her name on them. The women, along with many of the youngsters, then joined together in singing for us two special songs in Katherine's memory. I was very honored by this display of gratitude and appreciation, and accepted the crosses to bring back to Minnesota, to give to Katherine's husband and family.

Toward dusk, the cows and goats were returning from their grazing pastures far from the villages. Mary entered the corral made of large brush and sticks and thorny bushes for gates. She milked the cow into one of several large hand-beaded hollow gourds the Maasai make for this purpose. We decided we had to be on our way in order to arrive at our lodging for the night before dark settled completely, but we assured the women we would return in the morning.

We spent the night at Crocodile Camp, only a short distance from the village. We gathered for discussion, then freshened up in our round huts before returning to the common open-air area to share our evening meal. The grounds were beautiful, with rocks carefully outlining the paths in the dusty red soil, towering baobab and acacia trees, and a full moon shining down everywhere.

We could see the Ruaha River, which runs alongside Crocodile Camp, shining in that silvery moonlight. Velvet monkeys sat in the tree branches above, and geckos rested on the walls of our huts. It had been an exciting day, but sleep eluded us, as there was so much to process from the day.

We returned to Kwale in the morning. The women were working in the large fields of onions, corn, and tomatoes. We could hardly believe the progress the women had made since the project started in 2006. They now had nearly ten hectares of crops planted in tidy rows. As the site was near the river, they had worked together with other neighbors to build a trough through which water flowed down to their planted crops. Although we had helped them purchase an irrigation pump several years ago, the size of their fields had outgrown the pump. The women were hoping to save enough money to purchase another one. We walked the rows and found some of the women hoeing and tilling the red soil.

We returned to the Namnyaki Primary School classroom to have a short visit with some of the other women. I wanted to talk with them about a book I had decided to write and to ask if they would give me permission to include their stories. "Absolutely," they responded. They told me that they had no secrets. Everyone in their lives knew how they lived and the oppression they faced. In their villages, everyone knew everything. This fact of life was part of their culture and I was struck by how different this was from life in the United States, where we keep many secrets from each other. Just to be on the safe side, I asked if each would be willing to sign a release so I could follow US law.

One woman raised her hand. "The only problem I have— what if I can't write my name?" I realized that they had not been in a position or needed to write their names for over a year. They came to sit by me one by one, and Richard's hand helped them write their names. Even the chief came to sign a release form, but he was able to write his own name without any help.

The following day, we drove two hours on the washboard road to Image Secondary School. When we arrived at the school, the teachers and students greeted us.

All of the Maasai girls gathered in one classroom. They first performed some beautiful chanting songs for us in the Maasai language. Then they were very still and attentive while we asked their names and checked them off on our lists. We discovered there were three new girls whose names were not on my list. We asked them to speak to us about any issues or challenges they were facing in school so that together we could work on them.

Elizabeth spoke first. She said that they were thankful for their education. It had been difficult to fit in with the other students, she told us, but things were working out better and they were interacting more with the others. She had learned how to budget her personal spending money for items such as sugar and soap. Previously, she had had no responsibility for this—it was her parents' job. She talked about the girls who had difficulties in school and suggested that trade schools would be a good option.

Then a girl named Mary spoke, saying that she was grateful for the school supplies and dictionaries we had brought. She said it was difficult for them when their unsupportive parents learned they had not performed very well on their exams. Apparently, the parents had celebrated their failures in the villages, since their failures meant they would return to be sold for cattle. This upset her. She wondered if there was a way that we could keep their grades private. We told her we would check into this matter and get back to her.

Another girl spoke up, telling us that it wasn't safe for the girls to be home in the villages during school breaks. Even if their parents had been supportive by bringing them to school, once the girl arrived home, the other parents in the village said things like, "She has had enough education. Let's marry her to someone." Other villagers also expressed jealousy, saying that a particular girl had had enough education. And she said that parents might plan surprise pre-arranged marriages that the returning students would not be able to resist.

We learned that the girls wanted to spend their break time volunteering for the IMAGE Project, teaching the young children in the villages—or they wanted to stay at the school.

Rachel then spoke, saying she was worried about passing the final exams. She wondered what would happen if she missed out by just one point, as some other students had. If that happened, she feared that all of her "dreams of giving back to her community would faint."

Efiki, a secondary student and a volunteer teacher at the Namnyaki Primary School during breaks, was committed. "I swear, no matter what happens, I will return to the Maasai villages with my education to help my people," she said.

Then one of the chief's sisters spoke. "I am studying hard and not fooling around," she said. Hers was the same message we'd heard from her brother.

We asked a few of the students if they would be willing to meet with us in a smaller group to speak honestly and openly about their educational challenges. To my surprise, eleven of the girls said they would be willing to speak with us. I found this quite amazing, as only three years earlier we had sat with the girls, but instead of talking, they sobbed openly.

Efiki was the first to speak. Eloquently and in excellent English, she thanked all of the sponsors for helping the girls. She said the idea of keeping the girls at school during break was very important. The school year began for forms one through four in January. Forms five and six began in February. They all had a one-week break at Easter, a one-month break in July, and two months in November and December. She thought it would be helpful to make it mandatory that the girls stay at the school so they could get extra help with additional classes. Perhaps they could go home to visit for a short time—but not for a month at a time. The dangers were too great.

We were interrupted by a phone call from Richard. He said he was "surrounded by Maasai girls and mothers" in his office and asked that we come back early to Iringa so we could interview some of them, as they were interested in enrolling in our program.

We ended our conversation with the girls by talking about roles and responsibilities. Since some had inquired if there would be assistance in paying their college tuition, I explained that it was the mission of the IMAGE Project to support them through secondary school. If, however, they studied very hard and had a chance at a college education, we would do all we could to connect them with other groups and people who might be able to help them continue with their studies. They all said they understood. I knew we had to keep the focus of the IMAGE Project on secondary school; if we were to spread our resources too thin, we might become unable to support other educational plans.

A young student named Sara told Tasiana that she wanted to meet with us alone. So we sat quietly with her for several minutes. She asked for help with the educational costs that her parents would normally pay, explaining that her father has been in the hospital for two years and that her mother had had to sell all the cattle to pay for the fees. They hadn't been able to find a diagnosis for him.

At first we questioned if her story was really true, but we later found out that this was the same man who traveled many miles to see me in 2004 and who had brought a goat as a gift for helping his older daughter with her education. Armed with that knowledge, we later informed her that we could help her with other school fees.

We brought the girls many books donated from a school in Minnesota. Each girl received three or four books. They were so excited to have some books of their very own. We encouraged them to share the books with other Maasai students when they finished, so that all would have an opportunity to utilize the same books. (The concept of a lending library is unheard of in a land where books are a valued premium and can easily be sold for cash.) We ended our visit by taking their photos for their sponsors and then prepared to return to Iringa.

Before we could leave, the girls gathered in the courtyard of the school and began swaying, singing, and dancing as only the Maasai can. They sang solemnly, with certainty and depth; they were fully grounded in the Maasai culture. It was a profound experience to be the audience for such an evocative performance. We wished we knew what the words meant. As we listened, we watched the sun descend closer to the pastel mountains that made up the backdrop to this beautiful scene.

Just when we were to depart for Iringa, a teacher approached us and asked Tasiana something in Swahili. I assumed he needed a ride to Iringa, so I was prepared to find a seat for him. Tasiana motioned for me to come to her and whispered that he had just received a call that his brother had committed suicide, leaving behind a wife and five children. It was a reminder to all of us that life is difficult and precious; many face overwhelming circumstances. Somehow, this put our work into yet another context. We were humbled by the sheer effort it took to stay alive, let alone thrive, in Tanzania.

After another two-hour, bumpy ride over dusty roads, we had barely walked into the door of the Lutheran Center where we were staying when Richard appeared with two mothers and two young girls in tow. We sat at a table in the dining area for privacy, and Richard began by asking the first mother her name. She kept her head down and her voice was too low to be heard. As the conversation ensued, her head was practically under the table. She sobbed quietly, gasping for breath, ashamed at what she perceived as begging. Her daughter watched with tears glistening in her eyes. Richard found it hard to understand the mother, so he hung his head down low beside the table to hear her.

He translated her difficult story to us from Swahili to English. She said that in 2008, because of a conflict between the government and the Maasai over their cattle, she and her family were left with nothing—not even enough food.

She went on to say that her husband had recently suffered a stroke. Although he would approve of her daughter going on to school, she expressed that she had lost all hope for anything. She was working as a laborer to get food for her family. We sat in numb silence after hearing her story. She was begging for her child to be given a chance for a different life. What mother wouldn't? She wanted us to take her daughter right then and there. So we agreed that we could sponsor her, although we had no plan for where the daughter would stay until school started. But we had learned from experience that things have a way of turning out.

Then the other mother started to tell her story. She had been in Kwale the day before, but without her daughter. She told us that her husband beat her regularly, so she lived in the bush. The daughter who was with her was fifteen, but to me she looked more like ten or twelve. She was petite, pretty, and looked vulnerable and innocent. The mother had learned that her husband was attempting to arrange for an early marriage of this little girl.

The previous night, she and her daughter had slept under a tree in the bush, near the vegetables and rice they were growing by the river. When she heard we were coming to Kwale, she said to her daughter, "Come quickly; we must go to where the Americans (or individuals from the IMAGE Project) are visiting."

"What will happen when you return to the village?" I asked.

"There is no future with my husband, so I will return to my former village," she said. "If you come to the place where I stay, you will find us in dirty clothes. It's not because we don't wash our clothes, but because we have no soap."

Turning to her daughter, I asked if she wanted to go to school. In a very small but clear voice she said, "Yes, I do. I remember the day that I graduated from primary school with pride."

Richard considered the situation, and said that the two girls could stay overnight at his home, and then we should take the girls to Kwale, where they would stay until we could get them into school.

The next morning, Richard and the two new girls came to meet our group on the second floor of the Neema Crafts Centre where we were enjoying a cup of fresh coffee. Neema Crafts Centre was—and still is—a beautiful place that transforms the lives of people with disabilities in Tanzania, by providing them with handicrafts training and employment. As I walked down the stairs, I wondered aloud if these girls had ever seen stairs before. They had not. One of them had never been out of the bush before and had never been to a large town such as Iringa, which is quite large for Tanzania. The girls told us that they would miss their mothers, but they were excited to be going on to a school where they would join other Maasai girls.

After lunch, we met with Paulina, one of the first students in our program. Paulina was now working at Neema Crafts

Centre as a physical therapy assistant in their physiotherapy department, and doing very well. She came to us to talk about determining how she could go on to gain additional education, this time in tourism. I had to explain to her that our mission was about getting girls through secondary school, but that I would try hard to find someone who could possibly help her reach her dreams. She had been struck by polio as a young child, and although she found it difficult to get around, she wore a pleasant smile at all times.

With her excellent English, Paulina has done very well for herself; her mother is understandably proud. She is an excellent example of the opportunities that await the Maasai girls we support. She has a career and is now saving money to be able to move into tourism, where she feels her heart will be happier.

Then two star students stopped by to visit. They were both attending government schools in Iringa due to their excellent grades. The IMAGE Project was also the sponsor of the sister of one of the girls, and she is now at Tumaini University in Iringa. It is such a pleasure to meet with students experiencing success through our project—I wish I could better convey the heartfelt gratitude they express to me, and the light that shines in their eyes now that they have control over their lives. Their dignity and beauty shine through, and it is a joy to see.

The following morning we left with the two new girls to do some shopping. We bought them each a mattress and some personal items before heading out for the dusty, bumpy road to Kwale once again. This time we had the pleasure of talking with them to find out more about their lives.

The older girl said that her father was happy that she was with us. He would have sold a cow to pay for her education himself, she said, but the cows were gone, due to a conflict with the government. Her dream was to become a teacher and return to her village to help her people.

Then we talked to the little girl whose mother lived in the bush, alone. She explained that her parents had separated a few years earlier; her father had fallen into the habit of arriving home in the evening after drinking too much and beating her mother. The little girl had tried to intercede, but in a few instances she, too, was beaten.

On the day the men came for the prearranged marriage, they left without her after a heated discussion, but she knew they would return that evening. That was when she and her mother left. Her uncle gave them bus fare to get to Kwale village. She did not want to marry an old man, she told us because if she did, she would be forced to a life of hardship like her mother.

As we continued on the road to Kwale, I couldn't help but think of the mothers who risked so much for their young daughters. Living as they were, with the fear of the unknown in the bush, they knew it was worth taking chances to do what they had to in order to get their daughters educations. Even though they lived on their own, with little societal contact, they somehow knew that education was key to better lives for their girls.

We intended to visit the government school on the way to Kwale, but when we stopped, the school was empty—no children, no teachers—only empty classrooms. Someone waiting for a bus told us that all of the teachers had been summoned for training for the upcoming presidential elections, so the students had not come to school that day.

Although a bit confused, we decided that surely there was something else we should be doing that day rather than going on with our intended plans. We knew things have a way of working out in the best possible way. So as an alternative, we drove five and a half miles further down the road to the Namnyaki Primary School at Kwale.

As we approached the school, we saw several older men standing under the shade of the large acacia tree. I recognized some of them as the men who had been at the meeting a few days earlier. We decided to take a seat in the classroom. The men immediately joined us and we started discussing the issue of primary school children having to walk so far to school, building a secondary school, and how they could support the girls. It felt like we were having a comfortable conversation with old friends—even though Tasiana was interpreting and roosters crowed in the background.

Then the women started to arrive one by one to join us. There was further discussion about the primary school children walking nearly five and a half miles one way to school. One man suggested that maybe we could build another school so that all of the kindergarten through third-grade children could stay in the village and not have to walk the long distance to school.

They then started talking about contributing toward building a secondary school to meet the particular needs of the Maasai girls. The chief said he would donate a cow (a value of $350). Another said he would donate two goats (a value of $30 each). Then a man who had never even attended primary school said he would donate three goats and would give a cow, if he owned any.

In that moment, I was once again amazed at the progress we had made since 2000, when we were unable to find girls who could even *dream* of attending school. In great contrast, ten years later, we would have nearly one hundred girls in our program.

Chief Salehe told us that we had only to "say the word" and he would call a meeting of all of the chiefs. Another man said he would check with the five families who lived by him; he felt certain that 100 percent of his neighbors would contribute some goats or cows to the effort.

Then Judith raised her hand with a question. "Would a new school enroll girls only?" she asked.

Tasiana explained to her that we were concentrating our efforts on lifting up the girls to a higher level. I knew that Judith was caring for her grandsons, so her question about who would be allowed to attend any new schools was at the forefront of her mind.

We went on to discuss setting up classes that would help girls with their English and basic study skills before they went on to take the entrance exam for secondary school. The women and men agreed they were ready to support these classes in whatever manner they could. Even the women said they would help financially by selling some onions and other crops for cash.

Tasiana explained that any new school would need a "narrow gate," with high standards for students to enter. At the end of our conversation we asked if there were any questions.

The chief said, "We have no questions because everyone is in favor of a secondary school for the Maasai girls."

Near the end of the meeting, Mary's husband, Mateyo, entered the classroom. When Tasiana explained to him the topic under discussion, he said, "I will make sure we have enough stones and bricks for the school."

At the end of the meeting, Tasiana entered her cell number into the chief's cell phone so he could call her to let her know how many goats and cows others would contribute. It was quite amazing to observe the common use of cell-phone technology in Africa, living as these villagers do, in huts made of cow dung and mud, with no running water or electricity.

The women stayed in the room a bit longer. They told us that they had held a meeting after we left on Sunday to discuss the milling machine they wanted to purchase. They knew the machine had the potential to change their lives, due to the income it would generate. And now that their fields were doing so well, they needed a bigger pump to reach more of the land. The milling machine would allow them to purchase the sorely needed irrigation equipment.

The women already had a plan. They knew where they would maintain it, as well as who would run it. They had also decided that everyone, including contributors to the communal fund being set up to purchase it, would have to pay to have their corn ground.

They were willing to contribute $130 USD if we could help them with the remainder. Donations from my friend Katherine Slaikeu Nolan's memorial fund and other donations would also contribute to this economic opportunity, making a difference in the lives of the villagers forever. The women said they would honor Katherine's memory by telling their children and grandchildren how a woman who never knew them wanted to help them in a land far from her own. We were overwhelmed by the beautiful gesture made by Katherine, and similarly, by the heartfelt and grateful response on the part of these Maasai women.

When it was time to leave the village that day, I thanked the women for being a safe place for the young girls on the journey toward gaining an education.

"I'm glad that God had chosen us," Mariam replied.

I could only smile—everything seemed to be so simple—when I was anticipating at least some minor challenges, given that we had just dropped off two girls for them to care for. Once again, the women were teaching me important lessons about life, faith, and how we need to trust that things will always work out the way they are supposed to.

The next morning, we traveled the dry and dusty red dirt road to the village of Pommern to visit the girls in our program who were attending secondary school there. As we drove the bumpy road, I could feel a peace permeate me. It wasn't until that day, at that moment, that I realized my life was coming back full circle to where I had started twenty years earlier, in the very same village of Pommern. I was driving along the same roads, observing the same ancient trees and the same stunning landscape—mountains framing the Tanzanian countryside—that had intrigued me so many years earlier.

As we drove into the village, we passed by the mission house that I stayed in twenty years earlier. I was also aware of the familiar beautiful scent of the eucalyptus trees as we turned on the road down to the school. My thoughts took me back to the days we were renovating the very classrooms where now the Maasai girls in the IMAGE Project were learning to read and write, gaining a chance for a much better future.

It was a moment of closure in my life, and I was overwhelmed. I said a quiet, personal prayer of thanks to God for placing me in this circumstance where I could work to effect change in the lives of the girls I cared about so much.

We approached the school. I recognized the classroom. Although the school was now much larger, it still had the same peaceful feeling about it. The recently hired headmaster took us into his office to offer us some hard-boiled eggs, a deep fried donut, and tea. As always, the warm hospitality was there, with the wonderful people sharing whatever they had with the travelers from America.

The headmaster explained that, although he was new to the school, he was working hard with the Maasai girls so they could enter the exam rooms with confidence. He was impressed with the girls' commitment to education and their involvement in the community.

"Every Sunday, the Maasai girls' choir performs under the direction of a new student whom you will soon meet," he said. "Quite a few of the girls in your programs are considered leaders by the school. These leaders can be recognized by the scarves they wear around their necks." He seemed genuinely interested in helping the girls.

Then the headmaster said, "I want you to meet a new student named Rachel"

Rachel came into the small room and proceeded to tell us her story, with Tasiana acting as our interpreter. By this time, I was growing quite accustomed to this arrangement. I also knew that, when someone said something in Swahili and

Tasiana shook her head in disbelief, looked at us, and said in English, "Oh, my!" we had to brace ourselves for the interpretation to follow. This translation was no exception.

Rachel stated that at thirteen, she was forced to marry an older man not of her choosing. At age fifteen, she gave birth to a baby girl. But life wasn't easy. The man did not give her enough food (sometimes none) and sometimes not enough to even produce breast milk for her daughter. After four years she left her husband and returned to her parents' village. But her parents turned her away. Her father told her that he had received three cows for her and now she belonged to her husband.

So Rachel departed with her little girl and went to the church for help. It was her only hope for survival. A very kind woman took Rachel and her daughter to her home. After awhile, she began attending the woman's church, where she joined the choir. The woman told the pastor about Rachel and the pastor brought her to this school. Her baby now lives with her grandmother.

"Presently, no one cares about my future, except the woman from the church," Rachel said. She was just finishing up her story when a light bulb went off in my head. Prior to leaving for Tanzania, an acquaintance of mine, Bob Goheen, had said that he wanted to do something very special for Mary, his wife, in honor of their anniversary. Bob was a retired high school band director and Mary was a middle school band and choir director. Bob decided he would sponsor a girl who was interested in music, in honor of Mary.

Up until that moment, I hadn't found a Maasai girl who fit this description. With tears welling up in my eyes, I knew this was no coincidence, and I told Rachel that her prayers had been answered. Someone was looking for her and now she was found.

I assured Rachel she would have a full sponsorship at the school. It was an incredible beginning and ending of a story for an inspiring young girl. A terrible chapter of her life was ending, and a beautiful new set of possibilities was opening up for her. And once again I was struck by the incredible, nearly inexpressible difference that sponsors make in the lives of these young women.

As we walked by the classroom I had renovated twenty years earlier, I had a moment to reflect on where life had taken me—and then the girls started arriving! They were so excited to see us, and the room filled with laughter and talking. We started the conversation by asking them about the challenges they were facing in school.

Rehema said that the environment was different than she had been used to. It was colder at night (I jotted a note to myself to get them some more blankets). They said that water was readily available to them, so they don't have to spend time hauling it in twice a day from the river. They were getting extra help from the teachers before the exams (which was wonderful to hear). The teachers' extra work helped nearly all of the girls improve about 30 percent on their grades that year. They were also excited that this school had electricity, which meant that they had more time to study in the evenings.

We asked if they had any ideas to share with us about how we could improve their education. All but one of the girls said they would like to stay at school during the school breaks and holidays, as many of them still faced early marriages and other challenges at home. However, when we mentioned that all the other girls from the other secondary school might join them here during breaks, they were very happy. Even a girl who earlier had said she wanted to go home during break changed her mind, saying she would rather stay after all, since her sisters would join her and she missed them.

The girls performed some beautiful songs for us, under Rachel's direction. I could easily tell that Rachel was a leader and was thriving at the school.

The girls showed us the dorm rooms they share with non-Maasai girls. They insisted on taking us to the waterfall near the school. Although it was not too clear how far the trip to the falls would be, we realized it was important to the girls, so we piled into the vehicle and started down the road. After a mile or so, we parked the vehicle. I looked down the cow path into a valley filled with lush greens and beautiful acacia trees. The girls were so excited to take us on this journey, and they sang as we moved quickly down the cow path to get ahead of the herds of cows and goats walking in our way.

We went deeper into the valley and turned onto an even smaller path that led us to a wooded area. I could hear the water hitting the rocks as we approached. They assured us there were no snakes in this area. Not completely relying on whether they knew this for sure, I carefully inspected each step I took. We walked on to have our photos taken with the girls by the falls. It was an unforgettable outing.

Then we set out to begin the journey back up the hill as the sun beat down on us. We decided to drive the girls back to the school, as it was too hot to walk. As we said our goodbyes, we left with a sense of knowing that these girls had a better chance than most—with inspired and devoted teachers who believed in them, with extra help at exam time, and with the friendships they had with each other.

As we left the small village, we again drove by the mission house where I had stayed twenty years earlier. It sparked a flashback memory of my life before I had ever visited Tanzania. In that same moment, I learned that the woman who had joined us in the car was going back to Iringa to attend her brother-in-law's funeral. Contrasts are no surprise in Africa. Just as suddenly as a thought appears, the next thought and impression quickly changes it. Life in these areas of Africa is teeming, and where there is life, there is death. A discussion then ensued about the kind of person her brother-in-law was in life. It seemed to do her good to have an opportunity to describe her relative, and I was glad we could give her an outlet.

Early the next morning, we started on our long journey back to Dar es Salaam to catch our flight back to the United States. We stopped at the government school that the primary children attended before saying our goodbyes at Kwale.

We were greeted at the government school by a Catholic sister (whom the young children called "Sista"), who seemed like a very kind woman who gave selflessly to the children. She was excited to share with us that the younger Maasai children were doing very well on their entrance exams into standard one, having completed kindergarten at the Namnyaki School. We also learned the school has nearly five hundred students, most of whom walked long distances to attend.

Sista said that it was difficult for the Maasai children to walk so far to school. Usually, she'd have the children stay after school to clean up, but she always allowed the Maasai children to go home when classes were finished, because she knew they had not eaten all day and had a long walk in front of them.

According to Sista, some of the youngest children were from homes located behind the mountains at a distance of eighteen kilometers. Some parents had made small houses for their children closer to the school, and seven-year-olds were living alone, taking care of their needs without parental involvement, cooking *ugali* (a hard porridge) for themselves in the evenings. Sista tried to get them soap and other supplies, but she could not afford to support them. She often gave them her own possessions, but their needs were too great for her to meet alone. We were shocked to hear this. The biggest challenge would be to help find places for these young children to stay.

She went on to say the children were intelligent, they understood her, and were well-behaved, good children. The ones who come from a long distance, however, often arrived late and so would miss three classes each day. Classes ran from eight in the morning to three thirty in the afternoon. At the time of our visit, she explained that some of the kids were "camping," so they could be near the school to prepare for their exams. She had asked the parents to contribute more to support the children, but the parents could not afford much either because of the drought in the area.

We inquired what effect arriving late and tired to school after a long walk, and being basically unfed, had on the children's learning. Sista told us that she had been trying to get them food, but she was struggling, especially from January to March, which are bad months for obtaining food. Whenever the school is able, between noon and one o'clock each day, the staff feed the children *ugali*. When she feeds them ugali, Sista remarked, the children's attendance is very good.

With nearly five hundred children in attendance, the school had only ten teachers, one of whom was blind and needed braille reading equipment. They had approximately one book for every twenty students, so the children had to take turns with lessons.

When asked about the young Maasai children from Kwale who attend her school, Sista said they were prepared, in that they recognized a classroom, they knew what a teacher was and what teachers did, they recognized books, and had some basic Swahili. They could, however, use a teacher attuned to the special needs of this group of students.

We decided it would be a good idea to have a Kwale teacher visit to see what it was like for the young children on an ordinary day. We found out from Sista that Efiki, a form-six student mentioned earlier, came to the school on her breaks to teach the kids. Efiki, and others like her, were already giving back to their community.

We told Sista that we appreciated all the important work she was doing under very difficult circumstances. She replied that the children needed a good foundation, and then the future would be easier for them. We made our farewells with Sista, and left the government school.

We then drove on to Kwale to say goodbye to our friends who were becoming so familiar to us. They were waiting for us at the school. As soon as we jumped from the vehicle, Mary said, "The women have a gift for you!" They led me into the classroom and huddled around me in a group at the front of the room. Mariam draped a deep purple Maasai cloth over my back and tied it in a knot near my shoulder. It was decorated with a thick white zigzag design, typical of these Maasai women. They said it was a symbol of their love and friendship. It was an honor to receive it, along with their kind and grateful words.

It's November 2010. I'm sitting on my porch in central Minnesota, far distant from the red soil and dry heat of Tanzania and from my initial visit twenty years ago. I am in a reflective mood as I look out the window waiting for the first snowfall. Once again, I find myself writing, but this time I am recording how much in my life has come full circle due to my work with Maasai women and young girls.

I've spent so much time searching for answers to life's perennial questions: *Why am I here? What is my life all about? What is my life's purpose?* I now realize that, although I still ask these questions, I have found some answers for myself.

Although your fundamental questions about the meaning of your life may differ, and you may experience your search for answers differently than I have, the most important advice I can share with you is to stay with your own questions and find your answers within yourself.

For a long time, I searched outside myself and found some helpful ideas, but none were satisfying until I listened to the voice within me. I needed to validate my own thoughts and ideas by enacting them in the world—really listening to and valuing myself.

When I listened to my own voice, I discovered that my purpose was to speak for those who have no voice. Of course, one must first listen before one can speak for another. The Maasai women in Tanzania must have been waiting for an

opportunity to be heard when they spoke. I will never forget hearing the first woman speak honestly and courageously
to us about her life in Kwale. She said, "As a Maasai woman,
I am treated like a sack of corn, tossed about this way and
that." If she could make such a declaration within minutes of
our arrival at the village, what else would come out as other
women found their voices?

I found that listening to myself and taking my ideas out
into the world, even a world ten thousand miles from my
home, also enabled other women to listen to and believe in
themselves.

My 2010 trip literally brought me right back to the same
school in the same village in Tanzania in which I first taught
English and renovated classrooms twenty years earlier. My
passage through those intervening two decades has been an
amazing journey and has brought me to this place. Along the
way, I discovered that surrendering my life to God has taken
me to places and introduced me to people I could never have
imagined.

Initially, I was without a concrete plan, other than to listen to the voice within and believe in myself enough to carry
out what I heard. By trusting myself to carry out the purpose and plan God set in front of me, my life has been richly
rewarded by the people I've met and the places I've been.

I could never have foreseen that I would be a small part of
something that would affect such change in so many people's
lives. My amazement must be similar to that experienced by
the young Maasai girls on their journeys, girls who, although
they can't initially imagine themselves at school, are able to
leave their villages bound for secondary school, thanks to
their treasured sponsors' assistance. And once they arrive,

they become successful in their educational efforts, planning and even eventually changing careers. I feel that our lives—my life, together with the lives of my Maasai friends—have all come full circle to an unexpected and treasured place.

Although I feel there is closure on the journey I started twenty years ago, it also is clear that my journey with the Maasai women and girls, and with the IMAGE Project, has only just begun. The image that comes to mind is more of a spiral, similar to the designs used by the Maasai in the striking jewelry they make.

This work started as an impulse inside me, just a thought, similar to the small dot in the center of a spiral. By responding positively to the voice inside, that impulse has gone on to make larger and larger circles. While it has circled round, the work being done by the IMAGE Project is picking up momentum, gathering up people who are interested and committed to making a difference in the world. The lives of so many Maasai girls and women are evolving into something larger than any of them ever dreamed.

Yes, my journey has come full circle. But like the widening circles on the surface of water when a stone is tossed into a pond, the impact of educating young Maasai girls is ever increasing in effect. Together we dream of reaching full circle again.

Voices of Maasai Girls
and Women

A Collection of Letters and Stories

Your spear will be your pencil.
—Anna, a Maasai woman

Fear can paralyze us or move us to make changes in our lives.
    —Anonymous

Sara

Sara graduated from primary school in 2005 at the age of twenty, eight years later than most American students graduate. Her graduation is a miracle.

Earlier in her life, an aged Maasai man, heavily wrinkled in face and dressed in very old clothing, arrived one day in Sara's home village. Bringing six healthy looking cows with him, he approached her father. "Give me Sara to be my fourth wife," he said, "and I will give you these cows as her dowry."

Sara was milking her father's cows when her older sister informed her that the marriage negotiations were taking place. There was to be a ceremony and celebration that evening in a nearby house. When Sara heard about the event that would trap her forever, she hurried to her sister-in-law to ask for money for bus fare, so she could leave the area. Her sister-in-law agreed.

Racing through Sara's mind was the thought, *I could be eaten by lions or hyenas in the bush tonight, but I will take that risk rather than spend the rest of my life as a slave to an old man who will never love me or make me happy.*

She sneaked away around ten o'clock that night as darkness fell over the small village. Determined to escape, she ran as fast as her legs would carry her. She knew she would be punished if anyone learned of her flight. Her brothers would hit her with sticks until they tired. She remembered the unsuccessful escape of her sister, who was severely beaten when found. For fear of her life, her sister never tried to escape again.

Into the African bush Sara ran that night, taking nothing but her courage and the bus fare that would eventually bring her to the small town of Iringa. She had heard that some Americans were helping young Maasai girls go to school there. She dared not look too closely at her surroundings for fear she would lose her footing or fail to see danger lurking in front of her. But the greater danger she was leaving behind kept her focused on running until she was breathless.

Following the path others had made, she arrived at the main road as dawn was breaking. It was the road that would take her to a new life, a place she believed would give her choices and freedom. She didn't allow herself to think that leaving her village would mean she would never see her sisters again. She only knew she could not remain in the difficult confines of the village. She had to find a new life.

The bus came by the road once each day, and she made it just in time. After a long day on the bus, she arrived in Iringa late in the day. Searching for the nearest church, she pleaded for help. She related her story to many pastors before finding Dr. Richard Lubawa, who took her into his home that night and eventually enrolled her in school.

Due to Sara's good grades, she has been transferred to a different school. Her brothers learned of this through another student. "It will be easy to hijack her into marriage now," they said. But they never came.

Sara's mind is still haunted by thoughts of the old man that she was to marry: *he is a hungry lion—waiting, stalking me.* She stays with another woman in the city so she will not have to return home during breaks.

Sara continues to study hard today. She will graduate next year.

Regardless where they live in the world, mothers will take extreme risks, including the loss of life, if necessary, to help their children.

—Anonymous

Esupat and Nembulisi

Esupat lived her life as the second wife to the village chief. She was of little value to him and had no voice in family matters. She carried the burdens of famine, drought, and environmental crises. To say her life was difficult is an understatement.

When her first daughter reached the age of twelve, she was married off to a very old man. Esupat pretended it was okay, because her family had received five cows as a dowry. But when she listened to what was in her mind, she was conflicted. On the day her daughter left with the old man, Esupat's heart was heavy and filled with many unfamiliar emotions.

Although it was too late to save the oldest daughter's life, Esupat decided she would be willing to take drastic measures to make certain that the life of her second daughter, Nembulisi, would take a different path—even if it meant laying down her life.

As soon as Nembulisi turned thirteen, her father began discussing plans for her marriage. "We have no money; we cannot afford to send Nembulisi to school. What little we have must be used for soap, salt, sugar, tea—not education," he declared.

Esupat would not stand by this time and watch yet another daughter suffer the same fate. She knew what she had to do. Late in the evening, she sneaked out of the hut, secretly grabbing Nembulisi with her, urging her to be very quiet. Summoning every ounce of courage she had, she went directly to the acacia tree where she had stashed enough money for bus fare. Shaking with fear, she boarded the bus with Nembulisi, determined not to look back. Although a long ride loomed ahead, Esupat was restless and unable to sleep, knowing a severe beating would be her punishment when she returned to the village without her daughter.

Early the next morning, they arrived at the home of Esupat's mother, who had no idea they were coming. Yet her mother had instinctively felt that someday her daughter would come. She was all too familiar with the raw feelings that surface when a daughter is exchanged for cows.

She was also attuned to Esupat's courage, much like her own, and proud of the bold step she had taken. But her mother was also fearful of the suffering that would inevitably follow. She agreed to raise Nembulisi until she could find someone to sponsor her in secondary school. Together their mother-daughter bond would change Nembulisi's life.

Two years later, Nembulisi's grandmother heard that the IMAGE Project was sponsoring young Maasai girls for secondary school. Nembulisi passed the entrance exam, and four years later passed her exams into form five (similar to our twelfth grade)—an exam that only 25 percent of all Tanzanian students pass, let alone a young Maasai girl.

Today, Nembulisi dreams of becoming a heart surgeon. She is fascinated by the human heart in more ways than one. A smart, engaging, funny, and inspiring person to many, she is forever grateful for the risks her mother took to save her life and for the support given by her grandmother.

Maria

In the words of Maria, a mother of six children:

Many kids know how to read and write—they can even speak a little foreign language—English. I can now call myself a woman. I know who I am and I can think of ways to improve my income. I have learned how to read and write, even though not very excellent! I am no longer dependent on selling milk only. I can do business—grow and sell crops and make jewelry. I am a responsible mother! I can afford to give my children necessary needs. God bless those people who have been helping us.

Rachel

My name is Rachel. I have no mother. I thank God for all people who have been supporting and taking care of me in my education! I am now a graduate of primary school. I hope to continue with secondary education, and I am sure I will pass my exams with God's power! The IMAGE Project is a very big source of hope in my life! It has rescued me from early marriage and given me a chance to prepare for a better future. Please send my thanks to everyone in The Project!

Mariam

I am Mariam—an old Maasai woman. Even though I did not go to school, I am very grateful to the IMAGE Project. It has made a great change in my life and that of my children! Even though my older children were married at a very young age, I am very glad for my two younger children, Jeska and Joyce. Jeska is now doing her final exam and Joyce is in form two (similar to our ninth grade). I am very proud of them. I am thankful the IMAGE Project rescued Jeska from getting married too young. Her father had already received cattle for her dowry four years ago! Without the kindness of people in the IMAGE Project, Jeska would now be a mother of two or three children and living a very difficult life. Thank you, God, for your work!

Nashipay

Married when she was fourteen years old, Nashipay is now twenty-two and the mother of three children. She shared her story with the IMAGE Project:

I have never gone to school. My dad never allowed me to go, because he wanted me to take care of the goats. I was married to a man not of my choice when I was fourteen years old.

The man has been so harsh to me and beat me almost every day. I have never experienced happiness in my marriage life. My sister, if you have ever heard about physical abuse, that is the kind of life I have been living since I got married. I can't say much on this. . . .

(Nashipay cried at this point in her story, but after a few minutes she was able to continue.)

Last month, the man beat me to the point that I can't even stand up. I had no help; I could only hold my kids and cry. One of my neighbors informed my mother, and after five days my father came and took me to the hospital. As you can see, I am still using some medicines that I got from the hospital and still my body can't work properly.

As a woman, I want my children to have a better life. I don't want them to suffer as I have. I want to go to school, get an education, and help my children. I don't want to go back to my husband.

From my neighbors, I heard about the IMAGE Project that helps Maasai women. I feel like God has heard my prayers, so I decided to come and speak my heart. Please help me! I know how to read and write, and I'm ready to start with adult education and thereafter secondary school. I will be so grateful and I'm sure I will make an excellent performance.

A letter from Namitu

My name is Namitu. I am fourteen years old. I am the third born in my family and the only one who has managed to reach primary school education.

After completing primary school, my father got mad and chased away my mother after beating her several times. My mother had to stay away from the family, sleeping in the bush. One night, my father came into the room where I was sleeping with my small sisters and grabbed me. Fortunately, I managed to release myself from him and ran into the bushes. Later on, I went back to check on my sisters and took them away. We traced where our mother was staying and decided to run away from our father.

In November, I was informed that I had passed to join form one (similar to our eighth grade) in one of the schools in the village. However, it is very difficult for me to go back to my father's home, because my mother cannot stay with him anymore. I do not have anybody who can pay for me to go to school. Fortunately, I came across a Maasai girl who is studying at Image Secondary School, and she told me of the program that is helping Maasai girls. I came to see Pastor Lubawa after walking a long distance from my home. The pastor told me to write my story and wait for an answer for a week or two.

I know I have the ability to do well in school, because in the primary school I did very well and that is why I was selected to join secondary school.

I request you, please, to help me go to school and promise to do well in my studies. I have a dream of being a teacher in a secondary school, or a lawyer. It is unfortunate that Maasai men do not give girls a chance to study. Please, I beg you to assist me.

It is me,
Namitu

A letter from Nasaru

I completed my primary education in 2007. I come from a polygamous family. My father had ten wives, including my mother.

My father and all the wives have to live on their own, together with their children. My mother never had a son who could also inherit some of my father's properties. Women are not counted as people to inherit cows and other properties.

When I was in standard six, my cousins began receiving dowry from other young men, so that they can marry me after completing my primary education. After finishing my standard seven, my mother decided to take me away from the village and run away from forced marriage.

My good luck, I met a young man who was schooling at Image Secondary School and had finished form four (similar to our eleventh grade). He told me of his school and that there was a program that supported girls from the Maasai tribe. He gave the name of the person who was coordinating the program, Pastor Lubawa. When I hear of this, I found that it was a miracle and so decided to write this letter to him and included my picture, requesting him to consider me in the program.

Please help me so that I can have an education so that I can help my mother so that she can live a better life. I do not have any other help. I wait with hope for your answer. God bless you.

Yours faithfully,
Nasaru

A letter from Nanyokye

My name is Nanyokye. My parents died when I was still young. Then my mother's sister took me and I stayed with her for some time. Then she also died and a friend of my mother's sister took me in her house. I came back to the village and thought of getting married, but my boyfriend was not faithful and I decided to look for school. I had nobody to help me. I lived a life of hardship and without hope for two years.

One day, as I was talking about my story of no hope to my neighbors, they told me to go and see Dr. Lubawa and tell him my story. Dr. Lubawa helped me enroll in school. The school has changed my life. Now I live with hope and I know there is someone who cares about me and gives me education. I feel safe and I dream to be a nurse in the future. I am doing well in school, although I have stomach problems. I rank sixth out of forty-eight in my class.

It is me,
Nanyokye

A letter from Nabaaya

My name is Nabaaya. We are eight in the family with three brothers and three sisters. I am the seventh child. Unfortunately, my father died from TB.

My mother is just a farmer. I began my primary education in 1996 and finished standard seven in 2001. I was selected to join secondary school in 2002, but because I failed to pay school fees, every now and then I was told to go home and look for school fees. This made me to fail to finish my school. When I asked my relatives to help me, they refused, arguing that there was no need in educating a girl because she will just end up being married by someone else and will not contribute anything to the family.

I have heard of this program that is helping Maasai girls get education. I know I can do well in my studies. I have waited for this opportunity for years, and I believe this is an answer to my prayers. Please assist me to join the school again. I promise to be a good student. I know by getting an education it will help me and also other people in the society. I would like to be a nurse. Thank you very much.

It is me,
Nabaaya

There is a power in each of us to create our own destiny.
—Anonymous

Nemaoi

For as long as Nemaoi could remember, she wanted to go on to secondary school after she finished primary school in Tanzania. Going on to secondary school wasn't something most girls even dreamed about. Their lives were unpredictable and challenging enough already.

When Nemaoi finished primary school and passed the exam into secondary school, she went to her pastor for advice. Nemaoi knew the IMAGE Project was taking young Maasai girls into secondary school and she was excited that this could be her opportunity.

But Nemaoi's father had his own plans for her life. Unbeknownst to Nemaoi, her father promised her in marriage to an old man who was going to give Nemaoi's father many cows as a dowry. When he found out that Nemaoi wanted to attend secondary school, she was severely beaten. Nemaoi's mother was distraught as she watched in horror her daughter's suffering. There was nothing she could do.

Nemaoi crawled from the village that night into the African bush. Her cries were deep. For three days she stayed in the bush. She didn't feel the cold as she lay on the damp, red soil, but she felt the powerful disconnect that one feels when head and heart are in misalignment. She prayed to God that she would die. Death would be a way out of a bad situation that could only get worse. Her dream was shattered and she felt she had no way out.

After the third day, her hunger for education was overcome by a real need for food and water. She went to a pastor's home, but he said he could not interfere. She walked to the Catholic Mission Center. A young nun listened to her story and offered to help her if she would sweep and clean the mission house. The missionary took Nemaoi to the IMAGE Project and she was sponsored. It was an answer to Nemaoi's prayers. She was one of the first students to be sponsored.

Today Nemaoi is in secondary school. She continues to be an inspiring, smart, and committed student. The IMAGE Project is proud that Nemaoi was one of its first students to be sponsored to attend secondary school. Her courage has opened doors for many young girls through her mentoring of younger students and her compassion for others. Because of her, the lives of many young girls will be better.

The IMAGE Project

An Invitation

If you are inspired by what you read in this book and want to learn more about how the IMAGE Project empowers Maasai girls and women in Tanzania, East Africa through education and economic opportunities, please visit our website at www.imagetanzania.org.

Conclusion

I haven't a clue as to how my story will end. But that's all right.
When you set out on a journey and night covers the road, that's
when you discover the stars.

—Nancy Willard

As I listened to their stories of oppression and observed their developing courage and boldness, the Maasai women and girls inspired me in my quest for life's meaning. I began to acknowledge the journey I was on, and how it had some similarities to what they needed to overcome. Unbeknownst to the Maasai women, I was actually walking alongside them in their stories, now knowing why we were brought together. We had some of the same work to do.

Today the answer is clear. These Maasai women and girls helped me discover my life purpose: *to speak for those who have no voice.* What began as a way for me to help them discover their voices has taken me on a journey of finding my own voice. The stories they have told have helped me shape my life. They have found their voice within their stories. I have learned to listen.

For the past ten years, these women have meddled with my soul, and I will be forever grateful.

About the Author

Debra's passion in life is to speak for those who have no voice. She graduated with a bachelor's degree in sociology from Mankato State University. She currently works as a paralegal and devotes her life to empowering Maasai girls and women in Tanzania. She is the cofounder and executive director of the IMAGE Project, a Minnesota nonprofit organization whose mission is to empower Maasai girls and women in Tanzania through education and economic opportunities. She has been traveling to Tanzania since 1989. She lives in Rush City, Minnesota, with her husband Gary, two horses, lots of stray cats, and a busy border collie named Jack.